Children of Poverty

Studies and Dissertations on
the Effects of Single Parenthood,
the Feminization of Poverty,
and Homelessness

Stuart Bruchey
UNIVERSITY OF MAINE
General Editor

A Garland Series

The Positive Influence of Bonding in Female-Headed African American Families

Dorothy L. Taylor

Garland Publishing, Inc.
New York & London
1993

Library of Congress Cataloging-in-Publication Data

Taylor, Dorothy L., 1938–
    The positive influence of bonding in female-headed African American families / Dorothy
L. Taylor.
        p. cm. — (Children of poverty)
    Includes bibliographical references and index.
    ISBN 0-8153-1127-3 (alk. paper)
    1. Single-parent family—United States. 2. Single mothers—United States. 3. Afro-
American families. 4. Juvenile delinquency—United States. 5. Attachment behavior—United
States.   I. Title. II. Series.
HQ759.915.T39 1993
306.85'6'08996073—dc20   92–38900
                                                                                  CIP

Printed on acid-free, 250-year-life paper
Manufactured in the United States of America

This dissertation is dedicated
to the memory
of my mother
Doris Reed Pitts Taylor

CONTENTS

LIST OF TABLES

LIST OF FIGURES

FOREWORD

to

The Positive Influence of Bonding in Female-Headed African American Families

by Dorothy L. Taylor

After a hiatus of thirty years, a great deal of "official" attention has been directed toward family values and the "quality" of family life. Over this period of time discussions on these significant topics have taken place continually in small community meetings of concerned citizens, but the plight of the United States' family has only recently reached the highest levels of government. This newly-found concern on the part of the government was undoubtedly influenced by the Los Angeles rebellion which inconsiderately took place in an election year. Although many of these discourses functioned as catharses to help alleviate the anguish currently felt in the United States about the inordinate amount of crime and delinquency, the deterioration of our families, and the loss of values on which we have always prided ourselves as a nation, to date there has not been a coherent policy or series of programs addressing these crucial issues. Dorothy Taylor's innovative research helps to fill that inactivity gap by providing a valuable blueprint for a new approach to a major contemporary social problem. She lays a solid, empirical foundation for ameliorative action which she eloquently describes in *The Positive Influence of Bonding in Female-Headed African American Families*.

Many African American professionals were shocked and dismayed when Daniel Moynihan released his devastating report on the African American family in the mid-1960s; a stereotyping, "benign racist" report that Sam Yette so accurately described in *The Choice: The Issue of Black Survival in America*: "Moynihan conjures up old sex theories and cites illegitimacy birth rates to demonstrate the weakness in the fabric of black family structure." Almost three decades later this stigmatization of an entire subgroup of Americans has persisted despite efforts by African American scholars to emphasize the point that, like any other families, it is the *quality* of African American family life that is important. Quality has little to do with quantity --a two-parent home can be more detrimental to its children than a single-parent household and a female-headed household can be more beneficial for its members than the traditional "nuclear" family.

Within African American families there is a long tradition of extended family support. Since Professor Taylor's primary research focus is the relationship between the behavior of children and the natural support systems unique to African American female-headed households, the positive influence of the African American extended family is buttressed by her acute descriptive analysis of "natural" support systems made up of parents, siblings, and significant others who influence the behavior of juveniles in African American households.

Equally important, Taylor takes an initial, meaningful exploratory step in her attempt to determine the extent of the influence of parent-child interpersonal interaction on a child's behavior, especially in families dependent upon public welfare assistance. In her treatise, Professor Taylor challenges the myth of destructive, dysfunctional African American families, particularly, female-headed Aid For Dependent Children families, by reporting that not only is there substantial bonding in these families, but also that the bonding tends to deter maladaptive behavior in African American children. She demonstrates that consistent discipline and acts as simple as sharing a meal together--nearly forgotten actions that nationally were once so commonplace--contribute to parent-child bonding and help to prevent delinquency.

The inestimable value of Professor Taylor's empirical research is that her findings offer a guide toward solving some of the structural problems in society that lead to dysfunctional families and the deviant personalities that result from those families. The problems of family values and quality of family life are certainly not peculiar to African American female-headed households. Ours is a society that for the past three decades has reflected a "me" generation concerned primarily with materialism and greed. For hundreds of years the African American family has demonstrated its strengths and resilience. Despite the continuous setbacks of poverty, racism, inefficient and inadequate public services endemic to their life experiences in this country, they are *still* families. The important findings of

Professor Taylor's research reported in this volume surpass the contemporary question, "What have you done for *me* lately?" It demonstrates what we, as a society, can do for *all* of our children. Taylor's research paves the way.

Coramae Richey Mann
Bloomington, Indiana

PREFACE

During the past 10 years, the growth of single-parent female-headed households has proliferated. Much of the research literature of the last decade has refocused attention on the role of the family in explaining juvenile delinquency. This literature includes much conjecture that conditions in African-American female-headed households, particularly those receiving welfare assistance, are conducive to the development of juvenile delinquency or chronic maladaptive behavior. Therefore much of the family and delinquency literature concerning these families is centered around the "feminization of poverty," a concept resulting from Daniel P. Moynihan's 1965 study of the black family.

The renewed research interest in family relationships and in the impact of family structure and functioning on family life has paid too little attention to whether the interaction of the parent with the child contributes to or deters juvenile chronic maladaptive behavior in African-American female-headed households. This study provides empirical data that attempt to distinguish more accurately those interaction (bonding) attributes which are associated with such behavior.

The current family and delinquency literature, which includes the study of single-parent homes and parent-child relationships, reveals a minimum interest in family life components, such as "natural" support systems, child supervision, parental affection, parent-child leisure activity, or the issue of trust.

In this study, social control theory was the guiding framework for deriving the measures of interaction between parent and child, and for testing empirically the relationship of the interaction measures and of the natural support systems of African-American female heads of households to juvenile chronic maladaptive behavior. The empirical analyses bearing on this topic are based on secondary data compiled from intake, progress, and disposition forms of 140 juveniles in the Early Attention Program of the Children's Aid Society in Detroit. The juveniles were referred to the agency between 1984 and 1987.

The bivariate analyses show several statistically significant relationships between interpersonal bonding variables and the maladaptive behavior of juveniles. The most prominent bonding factors were that parents contacted the agency willingly, were consistent in disciplining their children, and prepared and shared meals with their children.

ACKNOWLEDGMENTS

I wish to express my gratitude and sincere appreciation to everyone who contributed in various ways to the completion of this study.

I wish to acknowledge my indebtedness to my doctoral committee -- Dr. C. Ray Jeffery (The major advisor), Dr. Frederic Faust, and Dr. William Jones--for their cooperation, guidance, and assistance. Their help and encouragement have been very beneficial throughout the preparation of this paper.

Special thanks is extended to Dr. Bennie Stovall, the Executive Director of the Children's Aid Society of Detroit, and to the Society's Board of Directors for providing me with the essential data for conducting this study. I also thank Dr. Larry Gant for his support while I was collecting data for this study. Gratitude is also extended to Ms. Rhonda Stapleton and M. Carolyn Crawford for facilitating the case history analysis.

My sincere appreciation is expressed to Dr. Britt Patterson for his support and expertise in counseling and guiding me through the statistical phases of this dissertation. In addition, I would like to thank my typists, Ms. Margie Smith and Ms. Terri Miller. Further I am appreciative of the assistance from the panel of judges -- Dr. Juanita Doss, (psychologist), Dr. Michelle Reid (psychiatrist), and Mr. William Iverson (social worker) -- I consulted to select appropriate items for measuring the bonding between juveniles and parents.

I am grateful to my daughters, Adrienne and Sharon, for their constant encouragement and assistance during the lengthy process of this dissertation.

Recognition and a very special thanks must also go to my two beautiful grandchildren, Rachael and Tyrone, for their love and patience.

Without the understanding and support from my husband, Amos, this tremendous task would have been far more difficult. I will be forever grateful for his unselfish emotional and financial support during all stages of this study.

The Positive Influence
of Bonding in Female-Headed
African American Families

CHAPTER I

INTRODUCTION

The dramatic growth of the single-parent female-headed household over the past decade has been well documented. This phenomenon has been subjected to numerous controversial studies. The United States Department of Labor (U.S. Dept. of Labor, 1984a) informs us that between 1975 and 1985 the number of African-American female-headed households increased more than 50%. The present empirical inquiry will give attention to the relationship between female-headed households, natural support systems, and the behavioral maladaptation of children.

The 2 million African-American female-headed households documented in 1975 increased to 3 million by 1984. According to a report from the Labor Department's Office of Information and Affairs, by 1984 approximately "29% of female-headed families were headed by black women, 69% by white women, and 2% by Hispanic women".

A number of fact sheets prepared by the Women's Bureau of the U.S. Department of Labor (1985) focus attention on the economic and labor force positions of women and on the effect of related issues. One such fact sheet noted that families headed by females experience a poverty rate three times the rate of all families and five times that of married-couple

3

families. Furthermore, when race is taken into account, the rate is even higher. This fact sheet suggests that "more than half of the black families with female heads live in poverty, and 47 percent of all black children are poor"

Many criminological theories argue that a positive relationship exists between poverty and crime, such as Merton's anomie, Cohen's middle-class measuring rod and Cloward and Ohlin's differential opportunity (Shoemaker, 1984). These theories appear to be supported by reports on the growing number of African-American delinquent children. For example, a report by the National Center for Juvenile Justice (1985) states that African-American children are overrepresented in institutions for delinquents. With regard to this issue, however, Billingsley argued as follows:

> Although black children were overrepresented in institutions for delinquents, they were underrepresented in institutions for neglected and dependent children; only 8.4 percent of all children in institutions for the dependent and neglected were black, considerable less than their proportion in the population. It is possible, of course that some of the underrepresentation of black children in institutions for neglected children is due to the nature of the system itself and how it operates. Since, in general, institutions for neglected and dependent children are a shade superior to institutions for delinquents, there may be a tendency for black children to be more readily categorized as delinquents rather that neglected as compared with white children. (1968, p.568)

The *Juvenile Justice Bulletin*, from the U.S. Department of Justice's Office of Juvenile and Delinquency Prevention (OJJDP) (U.S. Dept. of Justice, 1988), states that African-American and other minority youths make up more than 50% of the juveniles in public custody institutions. *Children in Custody* (U.S. Dept. of Justice, 1987), states that 3,500 national public and private facilities provide care for more than 80,000 juveniles. A comparison of 1985 and 1987 census figures reveals an increase in the minority population from 25,809 to 30,128; African-American juveniles show the greatest increase over the 2 years, from 18,174 to 20,898 (U.S. Dept. of Justice, 1988).

Statement of the Research Problem

According to the U.S. Department of Justice, (1988), the number of juvenile delinquency cases handled by juvenile courts in 1970 reached 1,052,000. In 1982 the National Center for Juvenile Justice Statistics estimated a caseload of 1,292,500, which is considered to be the lowest number of cases handled by the courts since 1975 (National Urban League, 1984). This report, however, states that these figures represent only a portion of the youths actually involved in the juvenile justice system. It states further, as a conservative estimate, that almost 4,000,000 juveniles actually have had police contacts. During this period, from 1970 to 1982 an estimated 2,000,000 of the police contacts resulted in arrest, and 1,000,000 of these were referred to juvenile courts. About half of the 1 million youths referred to the courts received counseling and subsequently were released with no further action. The remaining youths were handled through some form of court hearing.

Since 1983 there has been a substantial increase in the number of juveniles held in public juvenile institutions. The capacity of these facilities increased 10% from 1983 to 1987. As of February 2, 1987, they housed 53,503 juveniles. It appears that with the increased number of juveniles in confinement and the possibility of a decreasing juvenile population, a larger proportion of the total juvenile population was institutionalized. The *Juvenile Justice Bulletin* reports that 208 juveniles per 100,000 were in facilities in 1987, compared to 176 per 100,000 in 1983 (U.S. Dept. of Justice, 1988).

A substantial body of empirical literature exists regarding the effects of family variables on juvenile chronic maladaptive behavior. (See Chapter II.) Much of the data, however, is atheoretical or is based on dated perspectives that no longer are recognized as relevant. A major result of the current increased interest in such behavior in the female-headed household has been the need to understand juvenile conduct.

The dramatic growth of single-parent female-headed households over the past decade is a well-established fact. In addition, there is much speculation that conditions in African-American female-headed households, especially those receiving welfare assistance, somehow are conducive to the development of juvenile chronic maladaptive behavior. The prior literature on these households failed to address many issues important to this debate. For example, too little attention has been focused on the interaction of the parent with the child in African-American female-headed households, and on whether this interaction contributes to or deters the development of juvenile chronic maladaptive behaviors.

Over the past decade, human service literature has begun to emphasize the importance of the individual's natural support systems for healthy functioning, as well as for crisis intervention (Baker, 1977). The importance of the natural support system is emphasized in correctional institutions as well as in society (Roberts, 1983). For the purpose of this study, natural support systems include the parents, siblings, or significant others living in the same household, who may have a positive influence on the individual's behavior. Natural support systems do not include the staff of any program, institution, school, or organization.

In light of several years' experience as a foster care worker, a probation officer, a family counselor, and an independent presentence investigator, I contend that youths from female-headed households have a better chance of not developing chronic maladaptive behavior if their single parents have access to the inherent strengths of their natural support systems, especially in crises. Information obtained from various crisis centers acknowledges that if single parents do not have natural supports, they cannot provide the youths with the support the youths need to alleviate stress and anxiety. If natural support fails, the social support network is approached. If that attempt is unsuccessful, the third and final attempt for relief is through involvement with human service institutions.

With the escalation of public concern regarding female-headed families and juvenile chronic maladaptive behavior, the research community must respond to these concerns by exploring and examining the various factors related to this problem. The results from empirical studies will provide the scientific knowledge necessary to replace speculation about what specifically influences the relationship between membership in such families and this type of behavior. The community at large (including churches, mental health professionals, courts, and the law enforcement agencies) must be informed about the explicit, empirically derived factors that influence such behavior in the African-American female-headed household. Only then can the agents of intervention enhance their ability to regulate and/or eradicate the problems of juvenile chronic maladaptive behavior in the community.

The existing sociological literature on the relationship between delinquency and female-headed households discusses several social control and economic elements. Previous conjectural and experimental investigations regarding this relationship were founded on social control explanations (Hirschi, 1969; Nye, 1958; Reckless, 1961). Many earlier criminological theorists argued that a strong positive relationship existed between poverty and crime (Cloward & Ohlin, 1960; Cohen, 1955; Merton, 1968). More recent writers have rejected an exclusive economic (strain) explanation and are turning again to social control as well as to economic explanations (Cernkovich & Giordano, 1987; Chilton & Markle, 1972). To date, however, there is no conclusive evidence that either economic factors or social control factors are more significant in the development of juvenile delinquency.

Purpose of this Study

The purpose of this research is to provide an analysis that will help increase the understanding of the factors underlying juveniles' participation in maladaptive behaviors. The focal point of this inquiry is to understand more clearly the relationship between female-headed households and juvenile chronic maladaptive behavior by exploring bonding factors related to the parent-child relationship, as well as the natural support system of the female-headed household.

The prevailing research concerning African-American female-headed households, their natural support systems, and the ability of the bonding between the parent and the juvenile to influence juvenile chronic maladaptive behavior has produced thought-provoking findings. It has not provided many decisive results, however. Additional research is required to refine the results of these studies. New investigations also are needed to describe the supportive factors related to female-headed households and their effect on such behavior in African-American families.

The study seeks to ascertain whether economic variables, bonding factors, and/or natural support systems are related to the occurrence of juvenile chronic maladaptive behavior. The principal approach taken here is to determine which of these bonding factors (social control variables) have the greatest potential influence on the juvenile's behavior.

The subjects selected for this study were 8 to 17 year-old youths who participated in a family service intervention program in Detroit. All of these subjects were processed through the agency between 1984 and 1987 for engaging in maladaptive behavior and conduct unbecoming to youths; all were living in female-headed households. The data for this project were drawn from a secondary analysis of the agency's rather comprehensive files on the intake, progress, and disposition of the selected subjects.

The goal of this investigation is to provide the professional community with sufficient conclusive information on the explicit factors that influence juvenile chronic maladaptive behavior in African-American female-headed households. This research will not end the controversy regarding economic strain versus social control theories in connection with family and delinquency. It may, however, produce fresh directions for future research.

Although the current literature on family interaction and attachment assumes prominent roles in social control theories of delinquency, it contains few bivariate or multivariate studies assessing factors related to female-headed households and their effect upon juvenile chronic maladaptive behavior in African-American families. The intent of this study is to distinguish more precisely the family interaction mechanisms associated with maladaptive behavior in such households. Clarification of the effects of specific factors in these families would be helpful in assisting social service workers, mental health professionals, and the criminal justice system in their efforts to use human services effectively.

As noted earlier, human service literature is beginning to note the importance of the natural support system in assisting family members in crisis, as well as the potential impact of this system on development of programs and the use of services. Examination of natural support systems in African-American communities reveals an inherent source of strength for individuals, which can be explored as a resource in the development of culture specific counseling or of service plans, programs, and policies (Nichols-Casebolt, 1988; Staples, 1985).

Organization of the Study

Chapter II furnishes a brief review of the literature on family relationships and delinquency. This overview includes the literature from which I derived some of the operational terms such as *female-headed household*, *natural support system*, and *chronically maladaptive child*. In addition, I discuss the extent of African-American female-headed households, the factors related to such households, and juvenile chronic maladaptive behavior in African-American families. Finally, I review the literature concerning the impact of family structure and functioning on delinquency. This review provides the context for this research.

Chapter III explains fully the theoretical perspectives that produced the empirical hypotheses for this research. Social control theory, the theoretical perspective of this investigation, supports the empirical analysis of the juveniles bonding factors and of the factors that interact to influence the behavior of juveniles in African-American female-headed households. In this chapter I state the hypotheses for this research investigation.

The Children's Aid Society's Early Attention Program, which provided the data for the project, is described briefly in Chapter IV. This program provides intervention services, counseling, and alternatives primarily for youths 8 to 17 years old. The research methods used in this investigation are detailed in Chapter V. I begin with a discussion of the design, which is followed by a description of the sampling techniques, the measuring instrument, the data collection procedure, the parental demographic variables, and the methods used to obtain the statistical results.

In Chapter VI I discuss the preliminary data analysis as well as the procedures used for data reduction. Chapter VII presents the findings; descriptive background characteristics are illustrated in tabular form. In addition, I analyze the outcomes of several cumulative variables (parental socioeconomic variables; natural support systems of single female parents, and interpersonal bonding factors) relative to juveniles chronic maladaptive behavior and present them in tabular form.

Chapter VIII summarizes and discusses the conclusions and implications of the findings. In this chapter I place the findings of my investigation in the context of existing literature on family relationships and delinquency, and reveal the extent to which the present analysis provides insights into the factors that influence the behavior in question. I also discuss the methodological limitations of the investigation, present the implications for social control theory, and offer recommendations generated by this study for further scientific inquiry.

CHAPTER II

REVIEW OF THE LITERATURE

The examination of the connection between family relationships and juvenile delinquency has an interesting history. This investigation has been affected over time by the dominance of alternative hypothetical positions. Research into the relationship between family and delinquency lagged behind other areas of research and theory development because of the attitudes of scholars who held a criminological perspective, which minimizes the importance of family variables in comparison to peer, structural, and school variables.

In the late 1950s and the 1960s, however, after a 30-year interval, a renewed interest in the effects of family variables on delinquency, centering around broken homes and family structure, was introduced into family and delinquency literature. Since that time, researchers have focused on several major issues and have developed various sociological theories. Social control theories have contributed significantly to this renewed interest (e.g., Hirschi, 1969; Nye, 1958; Reckless, 1961). Nye (1958) proclaimed that sad, unfortunate, and dysfunctional homes were stronger correlates of delinquency than were broken homes. Hirschi (1969) reported that delinquency was related more robustly to parental attachment than to whether the juveniles lived in intact homes.

Initially the prevailing attitude regarding family and delinquency was influenced by Sheldon and Eleanor Glueck's (1950) *Unraveling Juvenile Delinquency*, which is considered one of the most prominent investigations in the history of criminological research.

Glueck and Glueck also conducted follow-up studies from 1956 to 1970. An assessment of criminological literature in the United States by Wolfgang, Figlio, and Thornberg, (1978) established that the Glueck and Glueck (1950) study was the most heavily cited research in criminology from 1945 to 1972. This research, however, has been largely rejected in contemporary sociological theories of crime. Glueck and Glueck's view that mesomorphy is a dominant predictor of delinquency, set forth in their 1950 research and in their follow-up studies, was unpopular among sociologists, who have a long-standing aversion to biological explanations of human behavior.

Wilson and Herrnstein's (1985) publication, however, was more supportive of this research; it suggested that Glueck and Glueck executed "one of the most detailed and comprehensive longitudinal and cross-sectional studies of male delinquency" (p. 175). Interestingly, however, Wilson and Herrnstein's publication also has been criticized severely for its concentration on specific components and its investigation of nonsociological variables (e.g., genetic predisposition) in the causation of crime. The Glueck study also was repudiated because of its focus on the family as the principal cause of delinquency.

In 1983 Hirschi and Gottfredson suggested that current theories of crime causation disregarded the significance of the family as an institution of socialization. Similarly, Bordua (1962) suggested that prevalent sociological thinking was willing to accept the view that delinquency is a reaction to stress only in relation to class structure, not to the family. He argued that sociologists and criminologists have disregarded or minimized much of the evidence that the family is related to juvenile delinquency because of their need to avoid "psychologizing." Bordua contended that criminologists would include structural and social variables (e.g., social class and peer relationships), but would ignore parent-child relationship variables and variables such as personality attributes because they are considered "too psychological."

Wilkinson (1974) supported Bordua's position by suggesting that the ideological bias in sociology and criminology was crucial in the acceptance or rejection of research on broken homes and delinquency during the past century. Gove and Crutchfield (1982) found that one of the most frequently duplicated discoveries in the literature was the considerable amount of evidence that family interaction is associated with juvenile delinquent activity.

Another study in this vein was conducted by Canter (1982), who focused on the effects of family factors on male and female delinquency. She noted that family normlessness was a more important predictor of juvenile delinquency than were other measures of family unity, such as parental influence or family prominence. Canter also pointed out that her study did not discover the expected gender differences in the importance of family bonds.

Cernkovich and Giordano (1987) specified interaction patterns in three types of families: two-parent, mother only, and mother/stepfather. Although they did not assess the family interaction elements in relation to structural consequences, their findings called into question the impact of family structure. They found that communication, identity, support, control, conflict, and supervision were related only weakly to juvenile delinquency when comparable interactions were observed within each type of family. This study concluded that family structure, exclusive of its effects on delinquency, was unrelated to patterns of dysfunctional family interaction.

Rosen's (1985) analysis incorporated structural factors such as single-parent homes, presence of father, social class, and family size. It included only two measures of functional factors: quality of father-son interaction and involvement with parent. Variables such as quality of supervision, conflict, and child abuse also were investigated. Rosen's investigation distinguished family structural and functional correlates, particularly for African-Americans. The most important factor for African-Americans was interaction with the father; factors pertaining to family size, presence of father, and social class also were related to delinquency in this group. The relationships were less clear-cut for whites. In this study it appears that the broken home was not important for either group.

Gove and Crutchfield (1982) stated the following in their study:

The literature consistently indicates that (1) one-parent homes, (2) poor marriages, (3) lack of parental control, (4) ineffectual parental behavior (5) association with delinquents as opposed to nondelinquencts and (6) very poor parent-child relationships are associated with delinquency (however it is defined). All of these factors influencing delinquency have in common that they are likely to be a consequence of parental behavior, with parental behavior being causally linked to a lack of effective role models, a lack of a "natural" home environment and a lack of parental supervision. (p. 304)

Gove and Crutchfield recognized that not many researchers are noted for their attempts to measure the type and quality of family relationships (Canter, 1982; Hirschi, 1969; La Grange & White, 1985), and that the extent of conceptualization and the measurement strategies usually used may not be sufficient for capturing the entire extent and the true quality of the relationships. They stated further:

It is time we start taking the relationship between family characteristics and delinquency very seriously and systematically determine the precise mechanisms of how family characteristics are related to delinquency. (p. 317)

Laub and Sampson's (1987) study, in which they reanalyzed the original Glueck (1950) data, has contributed to the literature on family and delinquency and also has supplied a revised assessment of Glueck and Glueck's criminological contributions. Their findings support Hirschi's (1969; Hirschi & Gottfredson, 1983) and Patterson's (1980, 1982) social control theories by indicating a direct relationship between family process variables and serious and persistent juvenile delinquency. This study also supports Loeber and Stouthamer-Loeber's (1986) study, which concluded that "aspects of family functioning involving direct parent-child contact" (p.234) were found to be the greatest predictors of juvenile maladaptive behavior and delinquency.

Similar family interaction variables (e.g., attachment, discipline, and supervision) were identified by Laub and Sampson (1986) and by Glueck and Glueck (1961) as the most consequential family correlates to persistent delinquency. Laub and Sampson's findings also showed that except for residential mobility, no structural background factors (e.g., household crowding, family disruption, economic dependence, native versus foreign birth, and mother's irregular employment) had any significant effect on delinquency. Family process variables, however, (e.g., father's and mother style of discipline, parent-child and child-parent attachments, and mother's supervision), "mediated some 80% of the effect of structural background on delinquency" (1986, p.20). This study strongly supports social control theories.

Over the past decade, a number of researchers have reviewed themes related to family (e.g., Herzog & Sudia, 1973; Loeber & Stouthamer-Loeber, 1986; Rankin, 1983; Rosen & Neilson, 1982; Rutter & Giller, 1984; Wilson & Herrnstein, 1985). These investigators generally believe that the research is ambiguous.

Their reviews point out that the relationship between broken homes and delinquency is inconclusive when official data are used in measuring delinquency and weak when self-report data are used. The outcomes also seem to fluctuate depending upon the sample size and the type of delinquent behavior (Nye, 1958; Rankin, 1983; Wells & Rankin, 1985; Wilkinson, 1980). This body of empirical inquiry is criticized in general for its deficiency in conceptual and experimental profundity (Wells & Rankin, 1986). A principal concern regarding this research, however, is its lack of efficacy in examining family situations that may be connected to family structure and to delinquency (Empey, 1982; Rosen, 1985; Rutter & Giller, 1984).

Free (1991) reviewed 68 articles and books published since 1972 which showed broken homes were more strongly associated with minor occurrences of delinquency than serious occurences. He also suggested that the correlation between delinquency and the broken home differs according to gender, race, socioeconomic status and neighborhood.

LeFlore (1988) examined the relationships of demographic variables, family structure (number of siblings in house, family intactness, sibling rank, and number of persons in household) and family environment (family relationship, personal growth, and family system maintenance) among 198 students (aged 10-18 yrs). Sixty-eight of these students were ajudicated delinquents. LeFlore used a discriminant analysis to determine which of the demographic and family environment variables had the most predictive power in discriminating between the groups. His findings indicated that 10 of the variables explained 49% of the variance between the chronic delinquent and nondelinquent groups. Personal growth was found to have the most discriminating power, followed by number of siblings, race, sex, and system maintenance.

Although the family and delinquency literature is not limited to the issues discussed above, my purpose here is to provide a brief review of the general family and delinquency literature before beginning a more detailed discussion of the literature basic to this investigation.

Literature on African-American Female-Headed Households and Delinquency

The conjecture that female-headed families, particularly those receiving welfare, produce more juvenile delinquents is associated most commonly with African-American families. Wilson and Herrnstein (1985) state that many persons tend to explain behavior mainly in reference to family processes, and that amazingly little is actually known about the effects of being reared in an African-American family, intact or broken. There is little question, however, about the difference between the structure and income of African-American families and of white families. Moynihan's (1965) report on the African-American family, issued to the government, stated that 25% of these families were female-headed households. By 1980 the figure had increased to 40%. During the same period, the proportion of white female-headed families also increased, but only by approximately 3%. In 1978, more than 50% of all African-Americans aged 18 and younger were living in female-headed single-parent households. Approximately half of these families were living in poverty (Wilson & Herrnstein, 1985). This finding addresses the "feminization of poverty," which not only is prevalent, but also is escalating rapidly. There can be no question that this is disproportionately an African-American phenomenon. In 1981, 6.9 million families were living below the poverty line; 30% of these families were African-American and 70% were female-headed (U.S. Bureau of the Census, 1981).

Some theorists continue to relate poverty to the increase in female-headed African-American families; others argue that among low-income groups, female-headed households remain much more common in African-American families than in white families. In 1977 two-thirds of all African-American families earning less than $5,000 a year were female-headed, whereas only one-third of all white household earning the same amount were female-headed (Spanier, 1980). Some scholars consider female-headed families to be a legacy of slavery. That point, however, is disputed by Guttman (1976), who demonstrated that African-American families were not disproportionately female-headed after slavery was abolished in the south. In fact, this was not the case as late as the first 20 years of this century (Guttman, 1976).

It appears that most studies which investigate the relationship between African-American female-headed families and delinquency tend to be as inconclusive as studies which investigate this relationship in families of all races. Some research findings show that living in a single-parent family is associated with a higher prevalence of juvenile delinquency among African-Americans (Anderson, 1968; Chilton & Markle, 1972; Clarke & Koch, 1975; Monahan, 1957); others find no such relationship (Robins & Hill, 1966; Rosen, 1970). Several of these studies were cross-sectional, comparing juveniles in broken homes with juveniles in two-parent households. Therefore little can be said about causality. Robins and Hill's (1966) study was longitudinal and retrospective; consequently it suffered from the typical problems of faulty memories, uncertain timing, and inadequate record keeping.

Few observational studies have been made. Hess and Shipman (1965) examined African-American mothers and their children in a laboratory, in the process of problem solving. They found that the lower-status mothers (those from lower socioeconomic backgrounds) spoke to their children less frequently than did the higher-status mothers. The lower-status mothers were much more authoritative while defining mother-child relations, and did not appear to give directions as succinctly as the higher-status mothers.

I believe that one of the studies most able to demonstrate possible theoretical links between family structure and juvenile delinquency is one in which a team of researchers has followed approximately 1,000 African-American children growing up in a predominately African-American section of Chicago for more than a decade (Kellam, Adams, Brown, & Esminger, 1982).

About one-third of these children live in female-headed households, another one-third in two-parent homes, and the remainder with mothers as well as various significant others such as live-in partners, friends, and other relatives. The children were classified by their teachers as "adapting" or "maladapting". The maladapting children were classified further as either aggressive or nonaggressive. Upon entering the third grade, the children from female-headed families were much more likely to be considered "maladapting" than those from other types of family, especially intact families. Upon entering high school, boys from female-headed families were more likely than others to admit to having committed various acts of delinquency. Family circumstances, however, were not the only consideration; it appeared that temperamentally aggressive boys exhibited troublesome behavior even though they were reared in intact families. Yet when no temperamental aggressiveness was identified, being reared in an intact home was connected with lower rates of self-reported delinquency than being reared in a female-headed household.

The data obtained from this inquiry have yet to be analyzed completely. Perhaps other longitudinal studies will establish that family conditions alone may be less crucial than the interactions of those conditions with temperamental traits.

The Kellam study appears to be the type of investigation needed to help resolve the question of the effect of household composition on juvenile behavior. The subject were identified shortly before birth and will be followed throughout their lives.

For several years the researchers will measure the connections between family structure, personality characteristics, and socioeconomic status.

Until recently, literature on African-American female-headed families focused mainly on the "feminization of poverty." More recent studies, however, argue that the structural conditions of American society are responsible for the status of the African-American family (Staples & Mirande, 1980). Blassingame (1972) included the concept of natural support systems (parents and significant others living in the household) when he argued that strong family ties persisted throughout the constant family destruction resulting from slave trade. Also, a landmark study by Guttman (1976) put to rest the myth that slavery destroyed the African-American family. Guttman contended that the family form of the past era had originated during slavery. This argument is akin to that regarding natural support systems.

In 1987, Smith reevaluated Moynihan's (1965) study. He reviewed and compared Moynihan's data with contemporary data on divorce and female headed families. Smith argued that the indices of family disintegration have become even more alarming since 1965 and concludes that the contemporary plight of the African-American family cannot be explained simply on the basis of race. He critiques the "strengths of Black families school" that applauds the crisis situation of Black families.

Although the Moynihan report served as a catalyst for focusing on African-American family "pathology," the importance of the natural support system in the African-American family, broken or intact, needed verification through sound empirical research. For more than a decade sociologists systematically ignored the issue of natural support systems and focused mainly on institutional support systems. In the late 1960s Andrew Billingsley, one of the most avid proponents of the strengths and resources inherent in African-American families, published a book that included several studies on this issue. During the past decade there has been a substantial increase in journal articles that mention the impact of family structure and function on maladaptive behavior, but the contribution regarding natural support systems in the African-American family has been less substantial. The following review will highlight some of the studies that have been conducted on this subject.

Literature on African-American Female-Headed Households and Natural Support Systems

In the recent past, economics has been cited as the most prevalent influence on African-American female-headed households. The early literature focused mainly on the "feminization of poverty", which was advanced in Moynihan's 1965 report to the government regarding African-American families and the fact that 25% of these families were female-headed. More recent studies, however, reject the economic theory. The authors argue that the structural conditions of the family, the concept of natural support systems, and interpersonal bonding are more significant in the relationship between delinquency and the African-American female-headed family (Billingsley, 1968; Cashion, 1982; Devore, 1983; Farnsworth, 1984; McGhee, 1984; Peters & de Ford, 1971; Staples, 1971).

Billingsley (1968) encourages social workers and other mental health practitioners to consider the resourcefulness and strengths of African-American families when developing service programs for African-American communities. He asserts:

> The black family should be looked at as a social system embedded in the black community; in turn, the black community is surrounded by the largely white community and its institutions. (p. 465)

Billingsley states that African-American families live in a different America, apart from the mainstream of the affluent society. He states further that African-American families fare worse than white families in this society. One of the purposes of his study is to explain why some African-American families function better than others.

According to Billingsley, a family's functioning may be related to two categories, the instrumental and the expressive. Instrumental functions pertain to providing the basic necessities such as food, clothing, and shelter, to receiving health care, and to developing occupational skills. Expressive functions refer to relationships with relatives and friends. These relationships can be intimate as well as complex.

Family members can relate to each other in ways that either enhance or deflate each member's self-esteem and sense of self-worth.

The subject of natural support systems falls into the category of expressive functions. Billingsley focuses on a series of studies which he argues are sensitive to family life in the low-income African-American community. These studies explain why some families function better than others; they include information pertaining to the natural support systems of families headed by single African-American females. The amount of empirical research on natural support systems may be limited because many researchers have focused on the feminization of poverty which, as mentioned earlier, is widespread, has been growing rapidly, and is disproportionately an African-American phenomenon (Wilson and Herrnstein, 1985).

McGhee (1984) furnished a sketch of African-American female-headed households for the National Urban League (1984), which was presented in their publication *The State of Black America*. As an explanation for the focus on this particular group, the author cites its rapid increase during the past 10 years and its intimate relationship with the poverty-stricken and disadvantaged members of our society. McGhee states:

> In 1970, 66% of black families were married couples and about 31% were headed by females with no husbands present. By 1980, the

percentage of black married couple families had decreased to 54% and female-headed families with no husband present had increased to 42%." (p. 43)

Much of the information contained in this paper was obtained from a nationwide survey of African-American households conducted by the National Urban League during 1979 and 1980. The survey, referred to as *Black Pulse*, was funded by the Carnegie Corporation of New York. *Black Pulse* data were collected by African-American interviewers in hour-long, in-person interviews of 3,000 African-American heads of households. Of these 3,000 respondents, more than 1,100 African-American females were heads of households with absent spouses. The survey included topics such as personal income and informal support structures in the African-American community.

In reference to informal support, McGhee reported that the relatives of 86% of the sample of households headed by single females lived in the same city, but not in the same residence. Of this 86%, 75% had weekly contact with their relatives, and more than 30% had daily contact. These statistics indicate strong family ties.

The survey results also revealed the existence of mutual support systems. Although the single female heads of households often used these systems, the situation was not unilateral but reciprocal. McGhee states the following in reference to mutual support systems:

Our data indicates that there is a broad-based informal system of reciprocal exchange of money, goods and services between black female-headed households and their relatives in other households. The system is broad-based because it includes all three commodities: money, goods and services. It is reciprocal because the flow is in both directions--single female household heads provided money, goods and services almost as often as they received them. (1984, p. 53)

In conclusion, McGhee says that this mutual support system is a characteristic of African-American families in general, and not exclusively of African-American female-headed households.

Peters and de Ford (1971) focused on the recent growth of female-headed African-American families. The purpose of their research was to learn about the patterns of interaction and functioning of these families, their living patterns, and their mechanisms for developing and enhancing their coping skills. The authors also were interested in understanding the durability of these families in spite of their association with poverty and neglect. In addressing the attitudes and values of African-Americans regarding the role of African-American women, the authors say:

The black single female parent is part of a culture which understands that a woman may be either co-head of family as wife/mother, or head-of-family as solo mother. Each or both statuses are possible for female adults, and black children are socialized accordingly. (p. 165)

Peters and de Ford argue that because of the historical background of the African-American family, it is understood and accepted that although African-American females marry and procreate, they may not be parents in an intact family. This argument is based on two facts:

> During slavery, the men were sold away from families. More recently, men were legislated out of their families when government funded welfare programs routinely denied financial assistance to the families of unemployed fathers. (p. 165)

Peters and de Ford conducted two to four interviews with each of 11 African-American single female heads of households in their homes. This sample represented a range from welfare recipients to professionals. The respondents' socioeconomic status, based on income, education, occupation, and lifestyle, ranged from working class to middle class.

In regard to natural support systems, this study showed that the older-middle class professional women in the sample earned enough to support themselves and three or four children. Their salary was their only means of support. This economic factor is related to natural support by the fact that the younger working-class women, living on public financial assistance and caring for three or four children, were also supported by family and friends. These mothers typically did not use day care centers, nor were they involved with community agencies except for Aid to Families with Dependent Children (AFDC). If these mothers became employed, they used their mothers, friends, and neighbors for child care and emergencies.

Peters and de Ford concluded with the suggestion that their exploratory research must be continued in order to provide information on how to cope with the demands of the single-headed household. They believe that the information would benefit other "American female-headed families, which are becoming increasingly prevalent in American society" (1971, p 35).

Cashion's (1982) study is the result of a review of social psychological research on African-American and white female-headed families conducted between 1970 and 1980. The purpose of this review was to appraise the strengths and weaknesses of these households and to offer suggestions for improvement in the lives of children in this family structure. Cashion suggests that the need for this research developed from the well-known fact that female-headed families are increasing. Some social scientists, such as Glick (1979), have predicted that by the beginning of the century half of all children below age 18 will live in this type of family.

Cashion addresses four concepts related to childhood socialization theory and female-headed households: Freudian and cognitive theories regarding child development through modeling, emotional adjustment and self-esteem, intellectual and educational achievement, and juvenile delinquency. She contends that the female-headed family provides a unique structure for examining modeling theory, which presently is undergoing serious scrutiny.

She further informs us that Barkley, Ullman, Otto, and Brecht (1977) reviewed 81 studies examining the modeling hypothesis, and discovered that 59 of these studies rejected the hypothesis that children identify with the same-sex parent and model behavior by that parent related to their identification (Maccoby, 1966). Cashion's review of Smith's (1970) research on learning theory showed that the adolescent obtain guidance from the parent perceived as more able to guide, whether that parent is male or female.

In reference to role-taking, Cashion's review of literature shows that researchers such as Barkley et al. (1977) agree that the degree to which a child models masculine or feminine behavior depends largely on whether the parent considers the behavior appropriate. Lueptow (1980) and others suggest further that:

> girls learn feminine behavior from fathers who expect feminine behavior, rather than from mothers who are feminine. Children thus respond to parents' expectations rather than imitate same-sex parents. (p.78)

Cashion's review reveals that in the 1970s, a great deal of research was conducted on emotional adjustment of children in female-headed families. These studies produced overwhelming evidence that once children adjust to the initial trauma associated with divorce, they are as emotionally well-adjusted as children living in two-parent families. Cashion states further that Herzog and Sudia (1970), who thoroughly reviewed research on female-headed families over the pervious 10 years, found no adverse effects on children living in this environment.

(The findings of that study, however, are not consistent with Hypothesis 2 of the present study; see Chapter III).

In regard to intellectual or educational adjustment, it is assumed that children of indigent families perform poorly in school and that children in female-headed households are usually indigent. Therefore, in Cashion's opinion, the challenge for researcher is to determine whether children in female-headed households perform as well as other children at identical income levels. Cashion says:

> Research which has compared children in female-headed families to other children at the same income level find that children do not suffer because the father is not in the home. However, research which has not controlled for income report children rate low in scholastic achievement when the father is not in the home. (1982, P.81)

Cashion's review of Austin (1978) and others reveals that juvenile delinquency has no association with the female-headed household, but is associated with poverty (Chilton & Markle, 1972). This statement is contradicted by Andrew (1978):

> The highest level of violence among male juvenile delinquents is found among males from large two-parent families and not from female-headed families. (p.82)

In conclusion, Cashion contends, the literature suggests that hypothetically children need not be exposed to same-sex or opposite-sex parents in order to develop appropriate sex-role conduct. Further, children reared in female-headed households can experience healthy emotional adjustment, high self-esteem, intellectual development comparable to that of other children of similar socioeconomic status, and rates of juvenile delinquency comparable to children of identical socioeconomic status, but in different family structures.

Farnsworth's (1984) study, which included a sample of 99 black male and female juvenile delinquents from low-income households, investigated the connection between various family factors and four types of self-reported juvenile delinquency. The family factors consisted of structural and functional components. The structural indicators were the size of the family, the parents' employment, and the father's presence in the household; the functional indicators were the juvenile's contribution to the family decision-making process, the quality of family activity, and the juvenile's closeness to the parents. Farnsworth also studied some environmental factors (e.g., population density). This researcher conducted separate analyses for the males and the females, which divided the sample model and necessitated the use of reduced-form model in which each model delineated a particular arrangement of family structure, function, and environment. It was not possible to examine the exact effects of single factors in this study.

Consequently the results met only limited methodological criteria, and focused instead on additional questions about the significance of the connection between the single-parent home and juvenile delinquency.

Mayfield-Brown (1989) investigated the family structure and support of 3,832 adolescent mothers and nonmothers (aged 15-19 yrs) drawn from a 1978 baseline survey of low-income adolescents who were eligible for the Youth Incetive Entitlement Pilot Program. Her finding revealed that becoming a mother during the school years created an abrupt transition to adult status. The variation in the status transition and the family supports were influenced by both race and age. Caucasian mothers were significantly more likely than African-American mothers to choose the pathway of early marriage, while Black mothers were more likely to continue to receive family support. Mothers were generally more likely than nonmothers to live apart from their families; however, African-American mothers were more likely to live with their families.

Summary

Even though the amount of literature devoted to the African-American family has increased substantially over the past 10 years, very little specifically addresses the relationship of natural support systems to juvenile maladaptive behavior in the African-American female-headed family. Although many factors are based upon conjectural inquiry, researchers still cannot offer definitive statements. When attention is given to this relationship, it relates more to the economic status of African-American women and their impact on the civilian labor force than to family issues. Two of the researchers reviewed here, however, Billingsley and McGhee, consider natural support systems crucial to the viability of African-American families, whether single-parent or two-parent households.

Several researchers argue that juvenile delinquency is not associated with female-headed families (Austin, 1978; Hennessy, Richard, & Beck, 1978; Wilkinson, 1974) but with poverty (Chilton & Markle, 1972). The highest level of violence among male juvenile delinquents is found among males from larger two-parent families, not from female-headed families (Andrew, 1978). Female delinquents report negative perceptions of their fathers but are no more likely than nondelinquents to come from female-headed families (Lang, Pampenfuhs, & Walters, 1976). Feminist attitudes among girls do not contribute to delinquency (Giordano & Cernkovich, 1979).

Effective solutions to juvenile chronic maladaptive behavior in female-headed African-American households will be feasible when researchers identify the factors determining the conditions in which such maladaptive behavior occurs. In addition, the existing literature on this problem is deficient in identifying the factors basic to the decision-making process in female-headed African-American households.

CHAPTER III

THEORETICAL PERSPECTIVE: SOCIAL CONTROL THEORY

In general, the empirical findings on the African-American female-headed household and the social and psychosocial perspectives pertaining to juvenile chronic maladaptive behavior seem to be consistent with social control theory, the theoretical perspective of this investigation.

Much of the literature on family and delinquency suggests that the development of hypothetical interpretations of juvenile delinquency received a great deal of consideration. The dynamics of peer group interactions, however, have been the focus of a substantial amount of criminological investigation (Giordano, Cernkovich, & Pugh, 1985), whereas family structure has been considered by many criminologists interested in consequences of family variables on juvenile delinquency (Herzog & Sudia, 1973; Loeber & Stouthamer-Loeber, 1986; Rutter & Giller, 1984; Wilson & Herrnstein, 1985).

The relationship between the family and juvenile delinquency has been studied in various ways. As discussed earlier, this investigation has been affected over time by the dominance of alternative theoretical perspectives. The review of the literature on criminality shows that research into this relationship lags behind other areas of research and theory development. The recent emergence of social control theory has reintroduced the importance of family variables for understanding delinquency, even though the status of the family in delinquency remains humble.

My theoretical considerations are related directly to social control theory. The theoretical framework of this theory generates testable hypotheses regarding the interpersonal bonding factors that influence the conditions in which juvenile chronic maladaptive behavior will occur in female-headed African-American households.

Social control theory appears to possess a structure that is capable of blending key components from different theories such as social learning, cultural deviance (i.e., subcultural and differential association), and structural functional theories. The social learning model focuses on the significance of the parents as reinforcers and as role models of socially acceptable behavior. Factors that influence the effectiveness of parental modeling and reinforcement are affection, availability, and supervision. Family conflict and supervision are more important than family structure in this model (Patterson, 1982).

Social control, subculture, and structural-functional theories all focus on norm violations as the central topic of investigation. They are based on the assumption of a conventional order that creates a clear definition of norm violations. There is a sharp contrast, however, between social control theory and the subculture and structural-functional theories regarding the role of deviant motivation in maladaptive behavior.

It is assumed in subculture and structural-functional theories that the difference between deviants and conformists is related entirely to motivation for deviant behavior. These theories therefore investigate why some people but not others acquire these motivations. It is assumed in the structural-functional doctrine that some people suffer stress due to certain structural conditions, which moves them toward norm violations and maladaptive behavior; the subculture philosophy assumes that people learn attitudes and values as a result of involvement in a minority subculture, which disposes them to deviant behavior.

In contrast, it is assumed in social control theory that norm violations usually are so attractive and so profitable that most people are tempted to break rules. Therefore one does not need to comment on motivation, but rather to explain why such a small percentage of the population submits to temptation and participates in norm-violating behavior. Social control proponents concentrate on this issue by asking what controls (Hirschi, 1969; Nye, 1958) or contains (Reckless, 1967) the majority of people from submitting to deviant motivation.

Three major proponents of social control theory are Hirschi (1969), Nye (1958), and Reckless (1961). Nye, focusing on family and delinquency, argued that most delinquent behavior resulted from insufficient social control. He used *social control* as a broad term: it included *direct control*, imposed by means of restrictions and punishment; *internal control*, exercised through conscience; and *indirect control*, related to affectional identification with parents and other noncriminal persons, as well as to the availability of legitimate means to satisfy needs (Liska, 1981; Shoemaker, 1984; Taub & Little, 1985; Vold & Bernard, 1986).

To test his theory, Nye surveyed 780 boys and girls in Grades 9 through 12 in three towns in Washington State. His survey instrument included questions about family life as well as items measuring delinquency. Approximately one-fourth of the youths were considered "most delinquent," and the remainder "least delinquent" (Nye, 1958).

Nye found that youths in the most delinquent group, who were given either complete freedom or none at all, had larger sums of money available than the other youths and were rejecting of their parents. They disapproved of their parents' appearance, moods, and morals. Youths whose mothers worked outside the home and who were rejected by the parents were slightly more likely to belong to the most delinquent group. In contrast, youths in the least delinquent group were significantly more likely to come from families that attended church regularly, did not move often, and were from rural areas. In all, Nye tested 313 relationships between youths and their parents. He found 139 to be consistent with his control theory, 167 not consistent, and only seven inconsistent (Nye, 1958).

In 1961, Reckless suggested a "containment" theory. He argued that all individuals are affected by a variety of forces; some drive them toward committing criminal acts, and others restrain them from committing such acts. Reckless argued that these forces include *social pulls*, which draw an individual away from accepted norms to delinquency and crime, as well as *biological* and *psychological pushes* from within, which drive an individual toward delinquency and crime. These pushes include restlessness, discontent, inner tensions, hostility, aggressiveness, need for immediate gratification, and rebellion against authority. Aligned against these urges are the forces of internal and external containment, which restrain the individual from moving toward criminality. External containment consists of effective family living and support groups, and includes a consistent moral standard, institutional reinforcements, reasonable norms and expectations, cohesiveness, effective supervision, and discipline fostering a sense of belonging and identity. Internal containment is the product of internalization and consists of self-control, ego strength, superego, tolerance of frustration, sense of responsibility, resistance to diversions, goal orientation, and the ability to find substitute satisfaction (Liska, 1981; Shoemaker, 1984; Vold & Bernard, 1986).

Hirschi, the theorist most closely identified with control theory, argued that we are all animals; therefore there is no need to explain the motivation for delinquency because we are naturally capable of committing self-serving acts. He further posed a comprehensive control theory: individuals who are bonded tightly to social groups such as the family, peers, and the school are less likely to became delinquent. Hirschi believed that four elements were necessary for bonding: attachment, commitment, involvement, and belief (1969).

Hirschi's findings showed that boys who were more closely attached to their parents were less likely to commit deviant acts. These attachments were measured by intimacy of communication, affection, and closeness of mother's supervision. This relationship held across social classes except when the father's history included welfare or unemployment. In addition, boys who were more delinquent reported more attachment to their delinquent peers. Furthermore, the higher the aspiration, the lower the rate of deviance, regardless of the youths' expectations. These supported the social control arguments regarding the significance of attachment, commitment, involvement, and belief. The discovery that peer attachment was related to an increased risk of delinquency was impressive. This finding, however, was not confirmed in Hindelang's (1973) replication, which otherwise reported findings similar to Hirschi's. Bahr's (1974) study also was largely similar to Hirschi's (Rutter & Giller, 1984; Shoemaker, 1984; Taub & Little, 1985; Vold & Bernard, 1986).

Some theorists contend that a major weakness of social control theories is the fact that "weak bonds and lack of restraints" alone cannot account for the resulting behavior formation. These theorists suggest a need for the additional idea that delinquent behaviors have "social meanings," whereby the "social groups" reward the behaviors upon occurrence. Within this structure an "integrated model" was suggested combining economic strain, social learning, and social control perspectives (Elliot, Ageton, & Canter, 1979). It has been suggested that although this model overall conforms to empirical findings, it is not easy to test (Rutter & Giller, 1984).

Another criticism is that although control theorists offer a compelling account which agrees with the data, the sociological versions have been charged with using vague concepts and employing several descriptions that appear to be a portion of the action which is being explained. In addition, although the correlates referred to as "self-control," "attachment," and "belief" seem to be reasonable indicators of delinquent behavior, these correlates do not explain how these characteristics are acquired and how they distinguish people.

The theoretical perspectives of social control theory can be conceptualized to some extent as extensions of the social psychological model. The Chicago School investigated the ecological and social control factors that produce an urban environment wherein social controls collapse. Contemporary proponents of social control theory investigate the procedure by which the decline of social controls results in norm violations. They hold that there are two types of social control, the inner and the outer. The inner controls, they suggest, are the rules of society that people internalize as their own. These controls restrain behavior because of the self-satisfaction that people experience when their behavior is compatible with the rules; incompatible behavior, on the other hand, produces guilt and results in self-condemnation and low self-esteem.

Once again, the difference between social control and socialization theories can be observed. Proponents of socialization contend that maladaptive behavior is a result of a subculture socialization, which conflicts with the conventional order; social control proponents argue that maladaptive behavior is the result of insufficient moral socialization. The latter group suggests that the outer controls are probable more important because once an individual is identified as a violator of society's norms, the social rewards in various segments of life, which are associated with a respectable public image, are jeopardized. Deviant behavior can cause the loss of jobs, respect of family and friends, and financial hardships, and can result in incarceration. Therefore social control theorists suggest that people conform to society's norms more because of inner and outer controls than because of an absence of deviant motivation. Several of the various social control theories which have emerged concentrate on inner controls (Sykes & Matza, 1957); many others focus on both inner and outer social controls, such as the family and the schools (Hirschi, 1969).

Although social control theory has been criticized as insufficient to investigate the bonding issue without considering the task of socialization (Nettler, 1978; Rutter & Giller, 1984; Wilson & Herrnstein, 1985), I believe that it has great potential for the development of both theoretical and empirical propositions. For this reason I have adopted social control theory as the basis for empirical hypotheses in this investigation.

Basic Concepts of Control Theory

Before relating social control theory to the specific hypotheses of female-headed households and juvenile chronic maladaptive behavior, I present a brief outline of social control theory and its elements.

Shoemaker (1984) and Nettler (1978) offer more extensive discussions of the following ideas.

According to Shoemaker control theories consist of three key concepts:

> *Containment.* The drives and pulls (forces in general) toward delinquency must somehow be contained -- that is, checked or controlled -- if delinquency is to be averted.

> *Self-concept.* This usually refers to an image, whether of one's place in society or of one's value to others or to society in general.

> *Social bond.* Essentially, this concept refers to the connection between the individual and the society, usually through social institutions.

Travis Hirschi (1969) conceptualizes the social bond as consisting of four parts: attachment, commitment, involvement, and belief.

> *Attachment.* The psychological and emotional connection one feels toward other persons or groups and the extent to which one cares about their opinions and feelings (the social counterpart of the psychoanalytic concept of superego or conscience).

> *Commitment.* The result of a cost-benefit approach to delinquency. It refers to the investments accumulated in terms of conformity to conventional rules (such as time, money,

effort, and status) versus the estimated costs, or losses, of investments associated with nonconformity. (A rational aspect of the social bond, the social counterpart to the psychoanalytic concept of ego.)

Involvement. Participation in conventional and legitimate activity. In a school, for example, it would include extracurricular activities such as school plays, clubs, organizations, and athletics.

Belief. The acceptance of a conventional value system. In the logic of control theory, it is argued that a weakening of conventional beliefs, for whatever reason, increases the chances of delinquency. (Shoemaker, 1984, pp. 156-162)

Assumptions of Control Theory

The basic assumptions of control theory are numerous. This inquiry, however, is concerned with the specific assumptions that are related to female-headed households and juvenile chronic maladaptive behavior. Accordingly I cite Nettler's assumptions, which are as follows:

Attachment to parents is strongly associated with lawful conduct among youths, and this relationship holds regardless of social class. Attachment to school -- liking schoolwork and being concerned about the opinions of one's teacher -- is also associated with resistance to delinquency.

Academic ability and school performance are among the important predictors of lawful behavior, and these factors operate quite apart from any reported "social disability: such as being shy, less than popular, or unathletic.

Attachment to peers is also important, but not in the direct way commonly assumed. Birds of a feather do flock together, but the birds that so congregate acquired their feathers before they flocked. Boys who have been otherwise immunized against delinquency are rarely attracted to juvenile gangs. Young men choose friends who have similar interests, and the corrupting influence of the adventurous gang is limited to boys with little attachment to a conventional career:

Involvement in conventional activities such as doing one's homework reduces involvement in self-reported delinquency. Conversely, the more time one spends "riding around" or "rapping with buddies", the more likely delinquency is. (1978, p.314)

The ability of control theory to produce practical propositions is crucial for research into the relationship between female-headed households and juvenile chronic maladaptive behavior. In the following discussion I will set forth the general hypotheses of social control theory and will indicate how well they can be related to precise assumptions about the topic under investigation here. The following list contains the general propositions and the specific hypotheses obtained from social control theory. The present study, however, will concentrate only on those hypotheses which relate to the relationship between female-headed households and juvenile chronic maladaptive behavior. These are as follows, according to Shoemaker (1984, p. 153):

Human beings, young and old, must be held in check, or somehow controlled, if criminal or delinquent tendencies are to be repressed.

Higher organisms require training if they are to behave socially. (Nettler, 1978, p. 307)
Homo sapiens is born only potentially human. If the potentiality is to be realized, if the infant is to develop into a recognizable human being, nurturing must take place. (Nettler, 1978, p. 307)
Social behavior requires socialization, Human egoism is reduced, and balanced with altruism, only as the organism is reared by parents and their substitutes and as it identifies with them and the moral codes they represent. (Nettler, 1978, p. 308)

Shoemaker also presents these pertinent hypotheses (1984, pp. 153-173):

Delinquency is to be expected, considering all of the pressures and inducements toward delinquency to which most juveniles are exposed.

Delinquency is a result of poor self-concepts.
A boy's positive view of himself provides insulation against the pressures and the pulls toward delinquency, regardless of social class or

other environmental conditions. People are conceptualized as being composed of several layers of drives, pressures, pulls, and insulators or buffers. All of these forces affect the individual simultaneously, and they come both from within and outside the person. The most important of these forces, however, is the interval insulator, the self concept.

Delinquency is the result of a deficiency in something, the absence of a working control mechanism.

The difference between personal and social control theories of delinquency lies in the assumption of social control theory that social bonds and attachments are a stronger protection against delinquency than are personality characteristics.

There is a general societal consensus concerning conventional beliefs and norms, especially as these are associated with various institutions in society.

There exists an inverse relationship between religion and delinquency: that is, delinquents are less religiously active than nondelinquent.
Delinquents come from broken homes significantly more often than nondelinquent.
An association exists between delinquency and a variety of family relationships.
Juveniles who are unattached to their parents are also disaffiliated with school.

The above propositions of the social control

perspective reflect its utility for explaining the relationship in question, and produce testable hypotheses. As a prevailing theory of human behavior, social control theory has the capacity to integrate dimensions that can be explained by more micro-level conjectures (Rutter & Giller, 1984). Thus, when one is moving from the specific to the general, it is necessary to proceed from micro-level theories or specific propositions to the general theory.

Social control theory, as a general-level theory, furnishes the necessities for micro-level theoretical integration as well as for generating empirically testable propositions. Many investigators agree that the social control theory of delinquency -- that a social attachment or bond to conventional activities and values restrains maladaptive behavior -- has received convincing empirical support. Social control theory also is considered one of the most promising theoretical explanations produced to date, regarding delinquency and juvenile chronic maladaptive behavior (Shoemaker, 1984).

Hypotheses

The assumptions provided for this inquiry were directed by the current literature on family and delinquency, by social control theories, and by the widespread public attitude that a relationship exists between female-headed households and juvenile delinquency. Much of the current literature has concentrated on the causes of delinquency.

In light of the overwhelming attention given to causes, it appears reasonable to offer a few predictions about some of the factors connected to this relationship. Consequently, I consider economic and interpersonal bonding factors. The points cited in the previous section are not to be regarded as causal factors, but rather as elements that seem to have some bearing on the relationship in question, and that may help us understand this phenomenon more clearly.

Social control theory is based on the assumption that social bonds and attachments are stronger protection against delinquency than are personality characteristics. The hypotheses generated from the social control perspective reflect the basic assumption that juvenile chronic maladaptive behavior is due to the absence of social bonding. The purpose of the present study is to evaluate this premise. Specifically, I will examine the following hypotheses:

> *Hypothesis 1:*   The majority of chronic maladaptive children from African-American female-headed households failed to bond with their mothers.

This hypothesis is supported by the existing family and delinquency literature, which shows a general relationship between bonding and delinquency: the greater the juvenile's bonding to the parental figure, the more strongly he or she is bonded to the parent's expectations, and consequently to conformity to the legitimate standards of the larger society (Hirschi, 1969; Rutter & Giller, 1984; Shoemaker, 1984).

Family and delinquency literature also discusses whether parental attachment is more important in restraining delinquency in single-parent homes than in two-parent families. Hirschi contends that the attachment is equally important in both cases. His data support the position that the juvenile is not "doubly" protected if he is attached to two parents. If this is true, it would explain why, contrary to the expectations based on direct control hypotheses, single-parent households are virtually as effective as two-parent households at controlling delinquent or chronic maladaptive behavior (Hirschi, 1969).

> *Hypothesis 2:* The majority of single African-American females who are heading households in which juveniles exhibit chronic maladaptivity are not afforded the inherent strengths of their natural support systems.

In order to evaluate these hypotheses empirically, I conducted univariate, bivariate and multivariate analyses. The principal objective of the analyses was to ascertain what factors (e.g., economic, in-home support, and interpersonal bonding) influenced the circumstances in which juvenile chronic maladaptive behavior occurs in female-headed African-American families. In the following chapter I describe briefly the Early Attention Program of the Children's Aid Society of Detroit, from which the data were gathered.

CHAPTER IV

THE CHILDREN'S AID SOCIETY AND THE EARLY ATTENTION PROGRAM

The Children's Aid Society was established in 1862 when a group of church women established "The Home for the Friendless." It provided temporary assistance and protection for "homeless women and helpless children"; since then the Society has provided families with life's "building blocks" and has rendered service to more than 270,000 distressed children and their families.

The Children's Aid Society is a private, nonprofit organization that helps to provide innovative services, training, and program evaluation in child welfare. Over the years, the agency has established a networking system with various other agencies, schools, organizations, public officials, and private lay people in their quest to improve the quality of family life in the Wayne County area. The Society's commitment includes family preservation and the advocacy of children. In keeping with that commitment, the agency provides a broad range of programs for identifying and mobilizing inherent family strengths.

The Children's Aid Society is funded by government agencies, the United Way Foundation, and various other organizational and private donors including the Skillman Foundation, the Office of Criminal Justice,

54

and Bowling Proprietors Association of Michigan. The Society offers three service areas: in-home services, placement services, and interdisciplinary services.

The in-home services include child and adult sexual abuse assault services, preventive outreach services, single-parent family life, and the early attention program, the focus of this research.

The Early Attention Program is family-centered and provides intervention for juveniles 8 to 17 years of age. The program includes services to first-time juvenile offenders and children referred from other sources such as school and family. It provides counseling and other forms of support as positive alternatives to maladaptive behavior. The Agency received 798 referrals for intervention service in 1986 and approximately 800 in 1987.

The Children's Aid society has a staff of 153 employees, which includes (among others) an executive director, a director of social services, a director of program development, 4 program managers, 16 unit supervisor, and approximately 50 social workers. Policy of the Society is determined by a board of directors composed of individuals who have been involved with the agency for several years.

This agency believes that children are our greatest source of wealth and that the family is the most essential and most important human institution. Since its inception in 1984, the Early Attention Program gradually has proved to be a worthwhile intervention strategy for juvenile chronic maladaptive behavior.

CHAPTER V

METHODOLOGY

In this chapter I describe the research methods used in this inquiry. I begin with a discussion of the research design and also describe the sampling technique, the data collection instrument, and the data collection process. In conclusion I discuss the statistical analysis procedures used here.

Research Design

Using the knowledge gained from experience in the field, from a panel of judges, and from the literature, I designed a 71-item instrument to gather secondary data from the files of the Early Attention Program (EAP). (See appendix.)

This study uses a cross-sectional, descriptive methodology employing secondary data. The inquiry was designed to explicate those bonding factors which have the greatest impact on juvenile chronic maladaptive behavior. I analyzed the extensive intake forms, psychosocial history reports, progress notes, communication questionnaires for juveniles and for parents, and case disposition reports (e.g., In-Home Service Intake Record, Early Attention Program Report). These reports are essentially interview records, which counseling staff members complete at the juvenile's initial referral to the Early Attention Program.

It has been proposed that the two principal survey designs are cross-sectional and longitudinal (Babbie, 1983; Levin, 1977; McClave & Dietrich, 1985). The cross-sectional design of this study restricted me to making observations at a single point in time. This design, however, permitted me to collect data on various factors related to female-headed households and juvenile chronic maladaptive behavior.

Levin (1977), Hagen (1982), and other researchers have given several reasons supporting my use of secondary data analysis in this inquiry. First is the economic factor: this particular kind of study permitted me to collect and use an enormous amount of data in a short time. In addition, secondary data are useful when confidentiality relative to the protection of the juvenile and the parent is an issue. This kind of investigation allows considerable anonymity (Babbie, 1973; Sellitz, Wrightman, & Cook, 1976). I did not consider the use of one-on-one interviews with juveniles and their single parents because of the time factor and because of the financial and personal requirements for such a study.

The literature also indicates a number of systematic limitations in secondary data investigations. First, Sedman (1960) argues that the investigation of human conduct, in contrast to animal conduct, is difficult because the investigator must use methods that allow an independent variable to be controlled before and after observations, so that the effect on the dependent variable can be ascertained. Jeffery (1977) contends that when researchers use secondary data such as questionnaires or official documents, they are indirectly investigating human behavior.

Second, readers should keep in mind that the data originally were gathered specifically for use by the Children Aid's Society's Early Attention Program; consequently, the degree of precision may be less than I would have wished. In this study, however, the case records contained the desired indicators regarding the bonding factors between juveniles and their parents as well as the parents' natural support systems.

Third, investigations transacted across time may be impossible because of changes in documenting practices of the agency or because of agency politics. Documentation was not problematic for this project, although some slight alterations were made. Interagency politics were more crucial in determining the sample size used here. The initial population size of 200 Early Attention Program clients was to be selected from the closed files accumulated between the date of the program's inception in 1984 and December 1987. There was no concern about the ability to obtain this number because as stated in Chapter IV the program processed 798 referrals for intervention services in 1986 and nearly 800 cases in 1987. Approximately halfway through the data collection process, however, my research was interrupted for approximately 1 month, because of concern about confidentiality in recording information on abuse. The resumption of data collection also was contingent on a time restriction. Therefore the final population size was determined by the time constraint, which made it impossible to collect data on more than 140 clients.

The final limitation in regard to secondary data is that a control group is absent. There is no way except by using an appropriate control group to ascertain whether any external elements other than those contemplated here influence juveniles' chronic maladaptive behavior. The outcome of the investigation would have been improved if a comparable group of juveniles with no agency contact had been available, with whom I could have compared the research group. It was possible, however, to divide the youths in this study into chronic and nonchronic groups. Regardless of the limitations associated with cross-sectional methodology, I considered this approach useful in light of the exploratory nature of this study.

Operational Definitions

Female-Headed Household

The most common definition of a female-headed household in the literature that I used in this research refers to a household characterized by the absence of the husband (McGhee, 1984; Savitz & Johnson, 1978). The definition of a broken home is quite similar: it refers to a household characterized "the absence of at least one natural parent because of death, desertion, divorce, or separation" (Rosen & Neilson, 1978).

Natural Support System

The definition used in this study includes parents, siblings, or significant others who live in the household and who may have a positive influence on the individual's behavior. Natural support systems do not include the staff of any program, institution, or organization. I refer to the sources of support as part of the structural system (Roberts, 1983).

Maladaptive Child

For the purpose of this study, a maladaptive child is any child who engages in a pattern of behavior that is sufficiently troublesome to warrant acceptance by the Early Attention Program (EAP). This behavior may be serious or nonserious. To be deemed chronically maladaptive, the juvenile must exhibit more than one type or occurrence of maladaptive behavior. Serious maladaptive behavior in a juvenile would be any behavior whose consequences would be criminal sanctions for an adult, and/or which might have a devastating effect on the juvenile's future. An example of the latter would be pregnancy; adolescent pregnancy has been observed to be a major problem in the United States today (Nichols-Casebolt, 1988). Table 1 shows first and second occurrences of maladaptive behavior in the EAP sample.

TABLE 1
First and Second Occurrences of Maladaptive Behavior,
Early Attention Program

First Occurrence

	N	%
*Shoplifting	06	04.3
Running away	15	10.7
Truancy	70	50.0
Disruptive behavior	04	02.9
Destructive behavior	02	01.4
Sexually acting out	10	07.1

Insubordination	06	04.3
Fighting mother	01	00.7
*Carrying a concealed weapon	01	00.7
Loitering	01	00.7
*Assault on classmate	01	00.7
Disregard for family	01	00.7
Abandonment of 2-yr.-old	01	00.7
*Sexual molestation	01	00.7
Provocative behavior	02	01.4
*Extensive criminal behavior	01	00.7
Leaving home without permission	01	00.7
School problems (nonviolent)	15	10.7
*Armed robbery	01	00.7
	140	100.0

Second Occurrence

	N	%
*Shoplifting	02	01.4
Running away	01	00.7
Truancy	14	10.0
Disruptive behavior	01	00.7
Destructive behavior	01	00.7
Sexually acting out	19	13.6
*Pregnancy	03	02.1
Insubordination	07	05.0
Fighting mother	02	01.4
*Other drug incidence	01	00.7
*Selling drugs	02	01.4
*Using Drugs	05	03.6
*Assault on classmate	06	04.3
*Extensive criminal behavior	02	01.4
Leaving home without permission	02	01.4

School problems (nonviolent)	07	05.0
Lying a lot	03	02.1
None Indicated	62	44.3
	140	100.0

* Considered serious in this study.

Introductory Phases of the Study

During the initial phase of this investigation, I contacted the Children's Aid Society. In a personal interview with the director of program development, I requested and read copies of the various intake and termination forms used by the Early Attention Program counselors. After inspecting and evaluating the types of questions and variables appearing on these records, I determined that the data collection forms used by the Early Attention provided the variables of interest to my research and that there was no need to consider other agencies. Therefore I formulated the investigative questions with the assistance of a panel of judges and a review of prior studies in the literature. While planning to begin the project, I held discussions with the agency's executive director, director of program development, and staff. Although the board of directors approved the research proposal at one of their quarterly meetings, I also held a personal interview with the board members regarding this project.

After obtaining approval from the board of directors, I met again with the director of program development to discuss the precautions needed to ensure the clients' anonymity and confidentiality. He told me that even though the executive director and the board of directors were interested in this project, they were also concerned about their clients' confidentiality. I provided the director of program development with a data collection instrument and thereby allayed his fears; with this he was able to convince the executive director and the board of directors that the use of the intake forms and psychosocial history forms would not create any embarrassment for the clients. Thus the research proposal was accepted. I further allayed anxieties about confidentiality by submitting a written statement guaranteeing that I would remain accountable for securing the clients' anonymity and confidentiality throughout this investigation.

Sampling

The subjects of this research investigation were 140 maladaptive juveniles who had been referred to the Children's Aid Society's Early Attention Program between 1984 and 1987. I studied this period because the Early Attention Program began in 1984. The fundamental purpose of the sampling scheme used here was to guarantee that at least 200 clients' records would be available. Therefore I created the sample group by choosing the clients to be included in the project as I read their case records. This inquiry was designed as a population study because no sampling of subjects was to be conducted.

The population under study was maladaptive juveniles and their parents. Generalizability was a problem in using a population of chronically maladaptive juveniles in the Early Attention Program because these juveniles may not represent the general chronically maladaptive juvenile population. They represent only one type. A substantial number of maladaptive juveniles in the general population, however, have not been labeled officially as chronically maladaptive or as juvenile delinquents because (for various reasons) they are not brought to the public's attention, the parents do not choose to seek assistance from social service agencies, or the juveniles' behavior has not been recognized officially by law enforcement agencies. Therefore the findings of this inquiry will reflect a specific population of maladaptive children, some but not all of whom have been labeled officially as delinquent.

Many of the investigators who have conducted research on family and delinquency have focused on the delinquent behavior (Hirschi, 1969; Laub & Sampson, 1986; Nye, 1958; Patterson, 1980; Rosen, 1985). Usually they studied these particular populations because of official verification that some form of delinquency or maladaptive behavior had occurred. Because it has been argued that drawing samples of juvenile delinquents from social service agency records produces systematic bias and prevents generalization of the outcome (Herzog & Sudia, 1973; Nettler, 1978), this study includes juvenile delinquents as well as children who have not officially been labeled.

Intake, Psychosocial, Progress, and Disposition Records

In this section I briefly describe and discuss the questions that appeared on the interview records. The records include (a) the in-home services intake record, (b) the Early Attention Program closing and six-month precinct follow-up report, (c) the record of family, (d) the communication questionnaire (for the parents), (e) the sentence completion form (for the juveniles), (f) an Eco-map, (g) progress notes, and (h) the disposition report.

In-Home Services Intake Record

This document solicited extensive identifying information on the juvenile and the parent. It requested information on the natural mother's natural father's, or other caregiver's legal names, their aliases (if any), and date of birth, race, marital status, addresses, and home and work phone numbers. This form also contained the date of referral and information on the referral source. In addition it included a space for family religious preference. Along with the request for the full name, sex, and birth date of the juvenile and siblings was a question concerning whether any of the siblings were placed out of the household. Another question addressed significant others living in the home; it requested each person's name, date of birth, and relationship to the children in the home.

The intake assessment portion requested information on (a) the presenting problem as stated by the client, (b) the service requested by the client, (c) the worker's assessment of the problem based on the caller's description of the situation, (d) social work involvement with a mental health agency, and (e) services recommended by the intake staff, with notes of any unusual or special circumstances. This section provided the age and race of both the parent and the juvenile, parental marital status, religious affiliation, natural support system, referral date and source, and type of incident of maladaptive behavior. From this section the natural support system variable was the only one used as an independent variable. Maladaptive behavior was the dependent variable; the demographic variables, referral information, and participation in some form of religious activity were used as descriptive and/or cumulative variables.

Early Attention Program Form

The information requested on this form included the case worker's case identification number and name, as well as demographic information on the juvenile and his or her family. In addition, it called for information on problems identified by the police. The final portion of this form contained a six-month follow-up report. This form supplied the economic variables which related to the possibility that African-American female-headed households receiving welfare assistance generated conditions conducive to juvenile maladaptive behavior.

Record of Family

This form tended to duplicate the In-Home Services intake record in regard to the demographic information. It also asked the client, however, to provide information on previous marriages and extended family members, which I deemed pertinent to this study.

Communication Questionnaire (for Parents)

This segment of the interview records requested information on communication and interaction between the juvenile and the parent from the parent's perspective. Using a Likert scale (5=always, 1=never), the parents were asked to answer questions by circling the number that expressed most accurately their true feelings about their children's activities, their communication patterns, and their level of mutual respect, trust, and other matters directly related to interaction between parent and child.

Sentence Completion Form (for Juveniles)

This portion of the records requested information from the juveniles regarding their thoughts and feelings, and was presented in sentence completion form. The juveniles were asked to elaborate on subjects including what they were proud of, their attitude toward school, their feelings regarding being loved, and several other statements about self-worth that I considered to be bonding factors. I used some of the interpersonal variables as independent variables, and the remaining psychosocial item as descriptive or cumulative variables.

Eco-Map

The eco-map is an assessment, planning, and intervention tool that charts the ecological system of the client's life dynamically. The boundaries of this system encompass the person and/or his family in the life space. This map portrays an overview of the family members in their present situation; it pictures the important nutrient or conflict-laden connections between the family members and the outside world, and demonstrates the flow of resources, or the lacks and deprivations. This mapping procedure highlights the nature of the contacts and points out conflicts to be mediated, bridges to be built, and resources to be sought and mobilized (Compton & Galaway, 1979).

This particular map requested information on the various systems that influenced the juvenile's life. It asked questions about the flow of the relationships (strong, tenuous, stressful) between family members and indicated the direction of the energy flow. The systems involved here are the family, the school, and community.

Progress Notes

This segment requested information about the type of contacts between the caseworker, the juvenile, and the parent, as well as about progress. It supplied the data on the juvenile's medical history and on whether the health issues were considered by the parent. The juvenile and the parent were asked to state whether or not they had experienced any alcohol or drug abuse. I used medical history to determine the parents' role in seeking medical and dental services for the child; I deemed this action to be an indicator of bonding.

Disposition Form

This final portion of the interview records supplied the data on the juvenile's case disposition. I considered information regarding disposition to be important in understanding changes in family interaction patterns during contact with the agency. The data from this form, were too irregular to use in this study.

Data Collection

As stated earlier, the data collection procedure consisted of a secondary data analysis of the interview records used by the Early Attention Program. I preferred this procedure to the mail and telephone survey and the one-on-one interview for several reasons. First, the secondary data collection process assures clients of confidentiality and anonymity. Second, because many of the standardized forms were completed by the counseling staff, the reliability and validity were increased. Third, the interview records largely included open-ended questions; thus they were adequate for obtaining the clients' feelings and attitudes about their situation and their conduct in relation to extremely sensitive and personal issues. Finally, the use of this process eliminated the difficulty of securing participants, which occurs in one-on-one interviews or mail surveys. After collecting the data, I examined approximately 20 files containing interview records. The initial review allowed me to assess the forms and confirmed that the data of interest were available.

Consequently I could maintain in their entirety the basic variables of concern, such as the economic and interpersonal bonding variables. A subsequent review showed that the kinds of answers supplied by the clients were very useful in helping me prepare the research codebook. Some of the variables selected for this research have appeared occasionally in the literature; others were contributed by myself and by other mental health professionals. Of the 71 items used for data collection, 15 were associated with the interaction between the parent and the juvenile.

The staff interview records from which the data were collected follow a basic, standardized design, which requires all juveniles referred to the program to reply to specific questions. All of the questions presented to the clients from the standardized forms have the same wording and follow an identical sequence. This design gives all clients the opportunity to be exposed to identical "stimuli," except in cases of differential interpretation.

The forms used by the EAP included both open-ended and closed-ended questions. The closed-ended questions concerned the local law enforcement agencies' and the juvenile courts' intervention into maladaptive behavior, the demographic characteristics of the juvenile and the parent, amount and source of family income, placement of juvenile upon case disposition, and type of case disposition. The open-ended questions were related to such matters as interpersonal relationships and were completed by the juveniles, the parents, and the caseworkers. Most of the items were open-ended.

Having determined the dependent variable (the recorded behavior of the child which resulted in his or her referral to the agency), I gave immediate consideration to the four following issues in the interview records (major themes are listed in parentheses): (a) What type of maladaptive behavior had occurred (serious vs. nonserious)? (b) Who was the referral source to the program (commitment and involvement)? (c) Did the single female parent have any significant others (attachment, involvement, belief, and natural support system) living in the household? and (d) What types of interactions existed between the juvenile and the female head of household (attachment, commitment, involvement, and belief)? I regarded the third and fourth questions as potential indicators of the factors influencing the occurrence of juvenile maladaptive behavior.

I collected the following variables for descriptive purposes:

The juvenile's history of involvement with other social service agencies and the juvenile justice system. For this variable I used a Likert scale consisting of nine categories: (1) Department of Social Services, (2) Protective Services, (3) Wayne County Juvenile Court, (4) Northwest Guidance Center, (5) Neighborhood Service Organization, (6) Catholic Social Service, (7) none indicated, (8) other, and (9) unknown.

The socioeconomic status of the parent and the juvenile. The socioeconomic variables of the parent that I determined on the basis of income were employment (employment, unemployment, and unknown) and source of income, which was broken down into the following categories: 01=interest income (savings, checking, dividends, real estate income, etc.), 02=employment income, 03=self-employment income, 04=AFDC (Aid to Families with Dependent Children), 05=other social service benefits (food stamps, Women, Infants, and Children [WIC]), 06=VA (Veterans Administration), 07=child support, 08=unemployment compensation, 09=Social Security, 10=other, 99=unknown and second source of income. The juvenile's socioeconomic variable was employment.

The demographic characteristics of the juvenile and the parent. The parent's demographic variables were race, sex, date of birth, education, marital status, and natural support system. Demographic variables for the juveniles were race, sex, date of birth, and education.

History of substance abuse for juvenile and for parent. This history was based on two categories: incidence of alcohol use for parent (yes, no, alcoholic, unknown) and for juvenile (yes, no, alcoholic, under the influence of alcohol during offense, unknown), and incidence of drug abuse for parent (yes, no, drug addict, unknown), and for juvenile (yes, no, drug addict, under the influence during offense, unknown). As stated previously, the interview records essentially were completed by the caseworkers, so that the accuracy of the data was increased. Fewer than 5% of the 140 cases had missing data on the economic variables and the interpersonal bonding variables. Yet because of the agency's request for discontinuation of the data on abuse, I could not continue to collect data on incident(s) of spousal abuse, type of spousal abuse, incident(s) of juvenile abuse, type of juvenile abuse, abuser's relationship to juvenile, and juvenile's and parent's alcohol and drug abuse. These variables were highly relevant as antecedents to maladaptive behavior. Therefore the absence of items diminishes the depth of this study.

In all, I gathered data on 71 items. Because of restrictions by the agency and the focus of the investigation, 5 of the 71 items were not used in the analysis.

Descriptive Variables

In addition to economic and interpersonal bonding variables, I collected data on the following variables: (a) demographic characteristics of the parent, such as age, race, and parental status (although this study concerns the single female head of household, the status variable was important in determining the number of unmarried parents); (b) parental socioeconomic status, (c) natural support systems of single female parent, and (d) involvement with other social service or mental health agencies.

I produced these variables from the literature on factors that influence whether juvenile maladaptive behavior will occur. For instance, it is important to know whether such behavior is more likely to occur in female-headed households that subsist on AFDC and have no live-in support system than in AFDC-supported female-headed households with live-in support systems. The literature suggest that many single parents lack a support system because of their isolation from family members, which results from embarrassment associated with their dependency on social services (e.g., AFDC). Some psychological issues for the female head of household are (a) her perception of herself in relation to her children, (b) her perception of qualities she possesses, and (c) her perception of what needs improving about herself, which influences her feeling of self-worth (Billingsley, 1968; Staples, 1971; Wilkinson, 1974; Willie, 1970).

　　　The incident(s) of involvement with other social agencies is another descriptive variable used in this inquiry.　Many female heads of families are of low economic status, which increases their association with social service agencies.　Assistance such as food stamps, general assistance, and especially Aid to Families with Dependent Children is widespread among female-headed households.　This fact is not very surprising because (as mentioned earlier) the literature also shows that the poverty rate in female-headed families is three times the rate in all families and five times the rate in married-couple families (U.S. Dept. of Labor, 1985).

Statistical Analysis

　　　The 140 seventy-one item instruments first were edgecoded. The data then were entered directly into the Michigan Terminal System at Wayne State University. The means of analysis was the Statistical Package for Social Sciences (SPSSX), Version 3.0. The techniques for analyzing the data included univariate analysis, bivariate analysis (using cross-tabulations), and multivariate analysis (again relying on cross-tabulations).

I examined the univariate statistics to ascertain the frequency, percent valid, and number of missing cases associated with each of the 71 items.

Bivariate analysis established subgroup comparisons, which include the dependent variable and an independent variable. Another component of bivariate analysis focuses on the relationship among the variables. This component, which uses cross-tabulation, was appropriate for this study (Babbie, 1983).

In the initial data check for discrepancies and consistency, I noted that considerable amount of data was missing in the items concerning parents' alcohol and drug abuse. For this reason I removed these items from the final analysis. Missing data on the interpersonal bonding factors, although minimal, caused me to reexamine the agency's records. I found that the respondents (in this case, parents) in some cases marked only the "yes" answers but left the "no" answers blank when the answer was "no". I made the necessary alterations to the data to adjust for this occurrence. (Later I will discuss the significance of these alterations.)

After cleaning and validating the remaining data, the first step in the analysis was the creation of several new variables. Table 2 shows the measures of the independent variables used in the final analysis. I recoded and collapsed some items to put the data on maladaptive behavior into a form more amenable to the types of analysis I was using (e.g., serious/nonserious; chronic/nonchronic). I recoded the items on the basis of first and second occurrences of maladaptive behavior, specifying the type of behavior, and collapsed these behaviors into serious and nonserious. (See Table 1.)

These two new variables then served as the foundations for two scales: the Maladaptive Behavior Scale (MBS) and the Chronic Maladaptive Behavior Scale (CMBS). The MBS measured the severity of the behavior; the CMBS pertained only to subjects who exhibited chronic maladaptive behavior. I collapsed the MBS further to identify each juvenile as either chronic or nonchronic in regard to maladaptive behavior. (This procedure is illustrated in Figure 1.)

The next step was computation of the univariate statistics on all variables. All of the "maladaptive" variables are shown in Table 3; in the next chapter I elaborate on these statistics.

TABLE 2
Measures of Independent Variables

Demographic Variables

> *Parent*
> Race and Sex of Parent
> Computed Age of Parent
>
> *Juvenile*
> Race and Sex of Juvenile
> Age of Juvenile
> Employment Status of Juvenile
> Educational Attainment of Juvenile

Parental Socioeconomic Variables

      Parent's Employment Status
      Parent's Primary Source of Income
      Parent's Primary Sources of Income
      Parent's Secondary Source of Income
      Parent's Secondary Sources of Income
      Educational Attainment of Parent
      Parental Status
      Parental Marital Status

Natural (In-Home) Support Variables

      Type of In-Home Support
      In-Home Support Relationship to Parent
      Does Parent Have Any In-Home Support?

Interpersonal (Bonding) Interaction of Parent with Juvenile

      Did parent contact agency willingly?
      Does the juvenile have a curfew?
      Does parent attend school activities?
      Does parent assist juvenile with homework?
      Does parent give juvenile one-on-one time?
      Does parent prepare and share meals with juvenile?
      Do parent and juvenile attend religious services?
      Is parent consistent in disciplining the juvenile?
      Does parent encourage participation in family decision making?

Is the parent willing to trust the child?
Does parent listen to and communicate with the Juvenile?
Is juvenile involved in cultural and ethnic activities?
Are juvenile's television and movies monitored by parent?
Is parent involved in juvenile's medical/dental program?

After examining the univariate statistics to determine the percent value and the number of missing cases, I cross-tabulated the dependent variables relating to maladaptivity with the independent variables to ascertain the relationship among these variables.

The bivariate and multivariate procedures concentrated on tables; each table was examined for significant relationships. Test of significance used chi-square. Sellitz et al. (1976) and Babbie (1983) instruct investigators who use bivariate and multivariate analysis in search of relationships between the dependent and the independent variables that the first step is to examine the chi-square to identify the statistical significance of the relationship. The next step is to look for the appropriate measure of association in order to determine whether a negative or a positive association exists between the variables. The appropriate measure of association for this data analysis is Kendal's tau.

The next step was the computation of the scale for interpersonal bonding factors (IBF) based on the 15 factors. I recoded the Likert-type factors into nominal "yes" and "no" responses (as noted in Table 6) to correspond to the other bonding factors which already had that form. The "yes" responses were given the value of 0.

In an effort to assess the validity of the IBF scale, I applied a procedure similar to that for constructing Likert-type scales: I added the sums of the responses to the items in order to obtain subjects' scores. I established upper and lower quartiles for these scores and assessed each item against quartile placement, using the interquartile t-test I found no nonperforming items; the result was a 15-item scale with a possible range of 0 to 15. Then I divided the subjects into four groups (IBFBY4) based on their IBF scores. Those in the lowest percentile (0-25%) showed zero or one IBF.

The upper quartile (75-100%) contained subjects with 7 or more IBFs present. I performed this procedure to revel any latent relationships between maladaptive behaviors and interpersonal bonding factors and to examine further those found previously to be statistically significant by the bivariate and multivariate contingency table analyses.

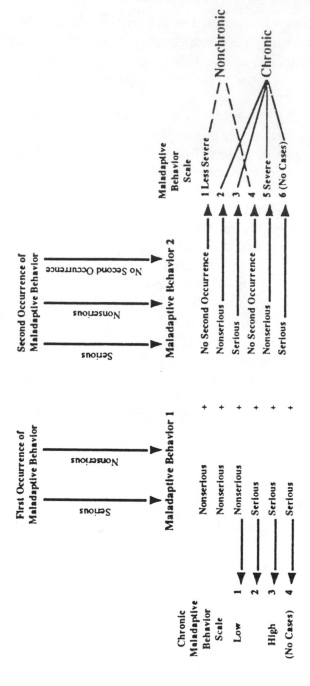

Figure 1. Steps in Deriving Maladaptive Behavior Dependent Variable

TABLE 3
Maladaptive Behavior Variables

Maladaptive Behavior 1

		Frequency	Percent
Serious		13	9.3
Nonserious		127	90.7
	Total	140	100.0

Maladaptive Behavior 2

		Frequency	Percent
Serious		23	16.4
Nonserious		55	39.3
No Second		62	44.3
	Total	140	100.0

Maladaptive Behavior Scale

		Frequency	Percent
Less Severe		57	40.7
		47	33.6
		23	16.4
		05	03.6
Severe		08	05.7
	Total	140	100.0

Chronic or Nonchronic Behavior

		Frequency	Percent
Nonchronic		62	44.3
Chronic		78	55.7
	Total	140	100.0

CHAPTER VI

PRELIMINARY ANALYSIS AND COMMENTS

The intent of this exploratory research is to determine which factors significantly influenced the conditions in which juvenile chronic maladaptive behavior occurred in female-headed African-American households. The primary question is whether the bonding between juveniles and their parents influences the development of chronic maladaptive behavior. A secondary concern is whether the female head of the family is afforded the inherent strength of her natural support system. This chapter describes the sample studied and comments on some of the initial univariate results.

The sample used in this research consisted of 140 maladaptive juveniles who were living in African-American female-headed households and who were referred to the Early Attention Program of the Children's Aid Society. The cases were distributed over a four-year period between 1984 and 1987; the greatest concentration was in 1986 (50%). Table 4 shows the distribution of these cases. The demographic and economic factors investigated here were the single parent's race, sex, age, employment, source of income, educational attainment, and parental status. I also

TABLE 4
Distribution of Sample By Year When Report Was Received (Referral)

Year	N	%
1984	02	01.4
1985	15	10.7
1986	70	50.0
1987	53	37.9
	—	—
Total	140	100.0

explored most of these characteristics for the juveniles, along with the number, age, and sex of siblings in the household. In addition, I analyzed the parent's natural (in-home) support system and the family's history of involvement with other social service agencies.

Descriptive Information

Of the 140 cases, 77% of the parents (N=126) were unemployed and approximately 23% were employed. The leading primary source of income for the parents (62%) was Aid to Families with Dependent Children (see Table 5). The second primary source was employment income (20%). The most frequent source of secondary income was Social Security, but the majority (83.6%) had no secondary income. In the educational data on the parents, a considerable proportion of items were missing (49%); most of those who responded (47.2% of the total sample) had no more than a high school education.

TABLE 5
Source of Parental Income

	N	%
Primary		
AFDC	87	62.1
Employment	28	20.1
Other	15	10.7
No source	10	07.1
	140	100.0

Secondary

Social Security	14	10.0
Other	09	06.4
No second source	117	83.6
	___	___
	140	100.0

Among those women who responded (N=136), 64% had been married at some point but now were either separated, divorced, or widowed.

The absence of a spouse in the home does not imply absence of in-home support, according to the definition of natural support used here. Although a large majority of respondents (75.7%) had no natural support, the remainder were noteworthy. Their natural supporters were divided almost evenly between relatives and nonrelatives. Figure 2 shows the breakdown of the natural support factor.

The parents ranged in age from 20 to 60, but only one was over 40; she was a grandparent rather than a parent. The median age for the parents was 38 years, with the greatest concentration in the 31 to 40-year range.

The juveniles' sex was distributed relatively evenly: approximately 49% were male and 51% were female. The juveniles ranged in age from 5 to 19 years, with a mean age of 13.7 years. (The EAP program was

Figure 2. *Natural Support Factors, Specific and Reduced*

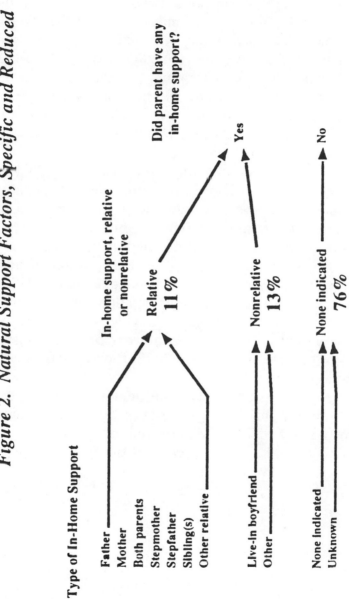

expanded to assist youths under age 8 and over age 17 in cases where the circumstances so warranted.) Most of the youths (57.9%) were between the ages of 11 and 15.

Only 4 of the juveniles reported that they were employed. This finding was not unexpected because most of the juveniles (84.3%) had an eighth-grade education or less. Alarming, however, was the finding that only 36.4% were at or below the average age of an eighth grade student. Approximately 59% of the juveniles had no prior contact with any agencies related to juvenile maladaptivity.

The items reflecting interpersonal bonding factors showed some interesting univariate statistics for maladaptive juveniles (see Table 6). I recognize that these answers are not extreme, but for the purpose of determining bonding I deemed it sufficient to place responses to these items in general positive or negative categories represented as "yes" and "no." With the exception of parents' participation in the juveniles' medical and dental care (roughly 97%), most of the factors showed that overall, interpersonal bonding factors were present in only about half or fewer of the juveniles' homes.

In regard to the interpersonal bonding factors (Table 6), only 54% (N=138) of the parents contacted the agency willingly. Almost half of the juveniles (48%, N=138) had a curfew. Most of the parents (69%,

TABLE 6
Percentage Distribution of Support and Bonding Factors

	Yes %	No %	Total N
Does parent have any natural support?	24.3	75.7	140
Did parent contact the agency willingly?	54.3	45.7	138
Does juvenile have a curfew?	52.2	47.8	138
Does parent attend school activities (PTO, etc)?	30.7	69.3	137
Does parent assist juvenile with homework?	13.9	86.1	137
Does parent give the juvenile one-to-one time?	30.0	70.0	140
Does the parent prepare/ share meals with juvenile?	30.0	70.0	140
Do parent and juvenile attend some form of religious service?	23.7	76.3	139
Is parent consistent in disciplining the juvenile?	15.1	84.9	139
*Does parent encourage juvenile's participation in family decision making?	28.6	71.4	140
*Is parent willing to trust the child?	46.4	53.6	140
*Does parent listen to and communicate with the juvenile?	44.3	55.7	140

*Does parent encourage juvenile's involvement in cultural/ethnic activities?	10.7	89.3	140
*Is parent involved in leisure activities with juvenile?	15.1	84.9	139
*Does parent monitor juvenile's television and/or movie selection?	21.6	78.4	139
*Is parent involved in juvenile's medical and/or dental care?	97.1	02.9	139

* Before collapsing, this was an ordinal-scale item.

N=137) did not attend school activities. Furthermore, 86% stated that they did not assist the juvenile with homework. Only 30% of the parents reported giving the juvenile one-to-one time. Interestingly, the same percentage reported that they prepared and shared meals with the juvenile. It was reported that (23%) of the families (parent and juvenile) attended some form of religious service. Discipline for the majority of the juveniles (85%) reportedly was not consistent. In addition, juveniles generally were not encouraged to participate in family discussion and decision-making processes. It was also reported that slightly more than half (54%) of the parents were reluctant to trust the juveniles, while fewer than half (44%) listened to and/or communicated with the juvenile.

It was reported that 85% of the parents did not participate in any leisure activity with the juveniles; an even greater percentage (89%) of the juveniles reportedly did not participate in any type of cultural or ethnic activity. Parents monitored television and movie selections, at least occasionally, in only 22% of the cases. Reportedly, however, they were involved heavily (97%) in the juveniles' health care.

The occurrences of maladaptive behavior included 29 different types (see Table 1), ranging from trouble at school to armed robbery. Truancy was, the most common first occurrence of behavior, exhibited by 50% of the juveniles. In this instance, truancy was either from home or from school. Sexually acting out predominated at the second occurrence (13.6%). A sizable proportion (44.3%) of the juveniles had no second occurrence of maladaptivity; they constituted the nonchronic group.

None of the bivariate tables resulting from the cross-tabulation of the interquartile T and the first and second occurrences of maladaptive behavior showed a high level of significance; even when they did so, the large number of cells caused the significance level to be invalid. These bivariate tables, however, indicated some relationships between more or less bonding and maladaptive behavior (see Table 7). In regard to the first occurrence of maladaptive behavior, the six juveniles exhibiting shoplifting fall in the middle range (2-6) of the interpersonal bonding factor scale (see Figure 3). Runaways fall on the lower end (0-3); approximately nine juveniles indicate less bonding. As for truancy, more juveniles fall on the marginally high (4-15) end of the interpersonal bonding factor scale, suggesting more (but only slightly more) bonding. Disruptive behavior also falls in the middle range (2-6). Sexually acting out appears to be distributed evenly between 0 and 15 factors. Oddly, however, school problems were predominately high (7-15) on the interpersonal bonding factor scale, a sign of more bonding.

Among second occurrences of maladaptive behavior, truancy falls in the low (0-3) range, suggesting that approximately eight juveniles experience less bonding. Sexually acting out also falls in the low range; this finding suggests less bonding, as would be expected. Six juveniles exhibiting insubordination fall on the marginally high end of the scale (4-15), surprisingly indicating more bonding; again, oddly, most of the juveniles (five) exhibiting nonviolent school problems showed a predominate large (7-15) number of interpersonal bonding factors.

I recoded maladaptive behaviors into two categories: serious and nonserious. Although "serious" behavior seemingly aligns itself with criminal activity, this was not the decisive factor; not all behavior determined to be serious (e.g., pregnancy) was criminal. For the first occurrence of maladaptive behavior, only 9% were considered serious. Forth-four percent of the 140 juveniles showed no second occurrence. Among those who did so (N=78), only 16.4% of the behaviors were considered serious.

TABLE 7

Relationship Between Maladaptive Behavior And Range

And Level of Bonding

First Occurrence of Maladaptive Behavior

	N of IBFs	Range	Level
Shoplifting	2-06	*Mid	Average
Running away	0-03	Low	Less
Truancy	4-15	**High	More
Disruptive behavior	2-06	Mid	Average
Destructive behavior	4-15	High	More
Sexually acting out	0-15	***Even	Even
Insubordination	4-15	High	More
Fighting mother	7-15	High	More
Carrying a concealed weapon	7-15	High	More
Loitering	4-06	Mid	Average
Assault on classmate	4-06	Mid	Average
Disregard for family	0-01	Low	Less
Abandonment of 2-year-old	7-15	High	More
Sexual molestation	4-06	Mid	Average
Provocative behavior	7-15	High	More
Extensive criminal behavior	7-15	High	More
Leaving home without permission	7-15	High	More
School problems	7-15	High	More
Armed robbery	2-03	Mid	Less

Second Occurrence of Maladaptive Behavior

Shoplifting	4-06	Mid	Average
Running away	4-06	Mid	Average
Truancy	0-03	Low	Less
Disruptive behavior	7-15	High	More
Destructive behavior	4-06	Mid	Average
Sexually acting out	0-03	Low	Less
Pregnancy	2-06	Mid	Average
Insubordination	4-15	High	More
Fighting mother	2-06	Mid	Average
Drug involvement	0-01	Low	Less
Selling drugs	0-03	Low	Less
Using drugs	0-03	Low	Less
Assault on classmate	4-15	High	More
Extensive criminal behavior	0-01	Low	Less
Leaving home without permission	4-15	High	More
School problems	7-15	High	More
Lying a lot	2-06	Mid	Average

* Marginal
** Marginally high
*** Evenly dispersed

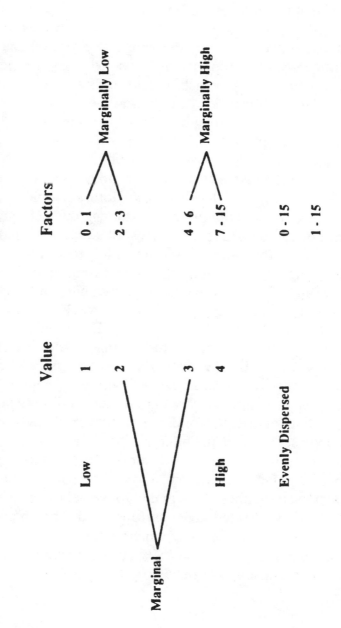

Figure 3. Range of Bonding and Maladaptive Behavior

The bivariate statistics further indicated a difference between serious and nonserious maladaptive behavior and levels of bonding. Table 8 shows that of the 13 juveniles who exhibited first occurrences of maladaptive behavior, the range of *serious* behavior is concentrated primarily in two to six interpersonal bonding factors, which would indicate less marginal bonding. Two serious cases, however, showed 13 or 14 interpersonal bonding factors. The nonserious behavior ranged from 0 to 15 interpersonal bonding factors, suggesting an even distribution of factors.

Sixty juveniles had no second occurrence, and five cases disappeared when the interpersonal bonding factors were computed. Among the 21 juveniles exhibiting second occurrences of serious maladaptive behavior, the range was primarily 0 to 6 interpersonal bonding factors, suggesting low to marginal bonding. Among nonserious maladaptive juveniles, interpersonal bonding factors ranged from 1 to 15, indicating a dispersion of bonding factors. These factors to be concentrated in the 0-to-6 range, and six factors appeared to be the average. When first and second occurrences of maladaptive behavior were combined, the serious juveniles had low to marginal (0-6) interpersonal bonding factors; this finding suggests that when bonding decreases, serious maladaptive behavior increases. The nonserious juveniles had more (0-15) interpersonal bonding factors, an indication that when bonding is dispersed evenly, serious maladaptive behavior decreases. I further divided the serious and the nonserious categories into a chronic/nonchronic scale. According to the data, more than half (56%) of the juveniles exhibited chronic maladaptive behavior.

TABLE 8

Bivariate Indication of Range and Level of Relationship

Between Interpersonal Bonding Factors and Maladaptive

Behavior

Maladaptive Behavior 1

	Frequency	Range, IBF	Level of Bonding
Serious	11	2-06	Marginal
	1*	13	More
	1	14	More
Nonserious	122	0-15	Evenly dispersed
	135**		

Maladaptive Behavior 2

	Frequency	Range,IBF	*Level of Bonding*
Serious	21	0-06	Low to marginal
Nonserious	54	1-15	Evenly dispersed
No Second Occurrence	60		
	135**		

---

*　Two serious cases showed high amount of bonding.

**　Five cases disappeared when interpersonal bonding factors were computed.

CHAPTER VII

FINDINGS AND EXAMINATION OF THE HYPOTHESES

This chapter presents detailed results relating to the hypotheses produced within the framework of control theories, particularly social control theory. Tables are used here to show findings on the factors that relate significantly to the conditions in which juvenile chronic maladaptive behavior occurs in female-headed African-American households.

Univariate, Bivariate, and Multivariate Analysis

In this investigation I used univariate, bivariate, and multivariate cross-tabulations to produce chi-square and Kendal's tau statistics. Univariate analysis examines only one variable at a time, as in Chapter VI, where I analyzed the subjects' background characteristics.

In contrast, bivariate analysis establishes subgroup comparisons that include both the dependent variable and an independent variable. Yet, although this comparison is also largely descriptive (in that it addresses subgroups separately) bivariate analysis involves an additional component: most of the bivariate analyses in this research also focus on the relationship among the variables. Whereas univariate analysis and subgroup comparisons concentrate on the description of the units

of analysis under investigation (e.g., people) bivariate analysis concentrates on the variables. Tables 9, 10, 11, and 12 contain these statistically significant items.
In constructing and presenting bivariate and multivariate tables, I report only the relevant summary statistics.

TABLE 9

Did Parent Contact Agency Willingly? by Chronic and

Nonchronic Maladaptive Behavior

		CHRONBEH		
Count Row Pct		Nonchronic 1.00	Chronic 2.00	Row Total
No	0	20 31.7	43 68.3	63 45.7
Yes	1	41 54.7	34 45.3	75 54.3
Column Total		61 44.2	77 55.8	138 100.0

TABLE 10

Is Parent Consistent in Disciplining the Juvenile? by

Chronic and Nonchronic Maladaptive Behavior

		CHRONBEH		
Count Row Pct		Nonchronic 1.00	Chronic 2.00	Row Total
No	0	48 40.7	70 59.3	118 84.9
Yes	1	14 66.7	07 33.3	21 15.1
Column Total		62 44.6	77 55.4	139 100.0

TABLE 11

Does Parent Prepare and Share Meals with Juvenile? by

Chronic and Nonchronic Maladuptive Behavior

Count Row Pct		CHRONBEH Nonchronic 1.00	Chronic 2.00	Row Total
No	0	38	60	98
		38.8	61.2	70.0
Yes	1	24	18	42
		57.1	42.9	30.0
Column Total		62	78	140
		44.3	55.7	100.0

TABLE 12

Bivariate Relationships between Interpersonal Bonding

Factors and Chronic Maladaptivity

	Chi Square	df	p	Tau	p	N
Did parent contact agency willingly?	6.39	1	.011	-.23	.001	138
Is parent consistent in disciplining the juvenile?	3.87	1	.049	-.19	.014	139
Does parent prepare and/ or share meals with juvenile?	3.31	1	.069	-.17	.023	140

Discussion of Hypotheses

The results of the two tests of hypotheses, conducted with bivariate analysis and univariate analysis, are outlined below. First I restate the hypotheses individually; then I present the statistically significant findings in Tables and discuss the results.

Hypothesis 1:   The majority of chronic maladaptive children from African-American female-headed households failed to bond with their mothers.

Hypothesis 1 suggests that a negative bonding relationship will exist between the juvenile and the single female parent.   That is, more juvenile chronic maladaptive behavior will be found when there is a lack of bonding or attachment between the juvenile and the single female head of household.

If the relationship is to be statistically significant, the critical value (alpha) must be $p \leq .10$, which is acceptable for exploratory studies (Babbie, 1983; Sellitz et al., 1976).

Tables 13 through 17 reveal that Hypothesis 1 is supported by the data. The test of significance shows a statistically significant relationship between the interpersonal bonding factor of (whether the parent contacted the agency willingly) and chronic maladaptive behavior for youths 11 to 20 years old (chi-square = 8.93 (1), $p < .01$). The negative association between the parent's willingness to contact the agency and juvenile chronic maladaptive behavior is moderately weak for 11-to-20-year olds (tau = -.29, $p < .01$).   Chronic maladaptive behavior was displayed by juveniles between 11 and 20 years of age whose parents did not contact the agency willingly. This finding indicates less involvement in trying to correct the child's problems than among juveniles whose parents contacted the agency willingly (44%) (see Table 16).

TABLE 13

Did Parent Contact   Agency Willingly? by Chronic and

Nonchronic Maladaptive Behavior, Unemployed Juveniles

	CHRONBEH		
Count			Row
Row Pct	Nonchronic	Chronic	Total
	1.00	2.00	
No 0	19	42	61
	31.1	68.9	45.9
Yes 1	39	33	72
	54.2	45.8	54.1
Column	58	75	133
Total	43.6	56.4	100.0

TABLE 14

Did Parent Contact   Agency Willingly? by Chronic and Nonchronic Maladaptive Behavior, African-American Males

	CHRONBEH		
Count Row Pct	Nonchronic 1.00	Chronic 2.00	Row Total
No 0	09 32.1	19 67.9	28 41.8
Yes 1	24 61.5	15 38.5	39 58.2
Column Total	33 49.3	34 50.7	67 100.0

TABLE 15

Is Parent Consistent in Disciplining the Juvenile? by
Chronic and Nonchronic Maladaptive Behavior, African-
American Males

Count Row Pct	CHRONBEH Nonchronic 1.00	Chronic 2.00	Row Total
No	0	23	32	55
		41.8	58.2	80.9
Yes	1	11	02	13
		84.6	15.4	19.1
Column Total		34	34	68
		50.0	50.0	100.0

TABLE 16

Did Parent Contact Agency Willingly? by Chronic and

Nonchronic Maladaptive Behavior, Juveniles Age 11

through 20

Count Row Pct		CHRONBEH Nonchronic 1.00	Chronic 2.00	Row Total
No	0	15 26.8	41 73.2	56 47.1
Yes	1	35 55.6	28 44.4	63 52.9
Column Total		50 42.0	69 58.0	119 100.0

TABLE 17

Relationships of Interpersonal Factors to Chronic

Maladaptivity, Controlling for Characteristics of the

Juvenile

	Chi Square	df	p	Tau	p	N
Unemployed Juveniles						
Did parent contact agency willingly?	6.21	1	.013	-.23	.004	137
African-American Males						
Did parent contact agency willingly?	4.52	1	.034	-.29	.009	67
Is parent consistent in disciplining?	6.09	1	.014	-.34	.003	68
Age of Juvenile (11-20)						
Did parent contact agency willingly?	8.93	1	.003	-.29	.001	119

I found a similar relationship for male juveniles. Those juveniles whose parents showed concern for their behavior by contacting the agency willingly showed less chronic maladaptive behavior (62% nonchronic) than male juveniles whose parents did not do so (32% nonchronic) (chi-square = 4.52 (1) p < .04; tau = -.29, p < .01) (see Tables 14 and 17).

In addition, unemployed juveniles whose mothers did not attempt to intervene by contacting the agency regarding their children exhibited more chronic maladaptive behavior (69%) than their counterparts (46%) whose mother did so (chi-square = 6.21 (1), $p <$ .02; tau = -.23, $p <$ .01) (see Tables 13 and 17).

When the parent's consistency in disciplining the juvenile was tested from chronic or nonchronic behavior, and when the juvenile's race and sex were controlled, it was revealed that among maladaptive African-American males whose parents were not consistent in discipline, chronic maladaptive behavior was more frequent (58%); when the discipline was consistent, however, nonchronic maladaptive behavior was much more frequent (85%). The chi-square value of 6.09 revealed the Hypothesis 1 is statistically significant at the 0.01 level ($p <$ 0.01) (see Tables 15 and 17).

When the parent's preparation and sharing of meals with the juvenile was tested for chronic and nonchronic behavior, and when the parent's employment status was controlled, a statistical significant relationship was found to exist between the variables (see Table 18). Table 18 shows that in the households of unemployed parents who prepare and share meals with their children, fewer juveniles exhibit chronic maladaptive behavior (nonchronic = 64%) than in the households of parents who do not do so (nonchronic = 40%). Thus Hypothesis 1 is both substantiated and statistically significant at the 0.05 level. The strength of this relationship between the parent's preparing and sharing meals with the juvenile, the juvenile's chronic or nonchronic behavior, and the parent's unemployment is revealed by the chi-square level 3.81 ($p < 0.05$).

TABLE 18

Does Parent Prepare and Share meals with Juvenile? by

Chronic and Nonchronic Maladaptive Behavior and

Unemployment

		CHRONBEH		
Count				Row
Row Pct		Nonchronic 1.00	Chronic 2.00	Total
No	0	28 40.0	42 60.0	70 71.4
Yes	1	18 64.3	10 35.7	28 28.6
Column Total		46 46.9	52 53.1	98 100.0

Juveniles whose parents are consistent in discipline tend to exhibit less (33%) chronic maladaptive behavior than those whose parents are not (59%) (see Table 10). In addition, the test of statistical significance revealed a chi-square value of 5.19, which makes Hypothesis 1 statistically significant at the 0.02 level (p < 0.02). Therefore the statistical significance shows that the parent's consistency in disciplining the juvenile has a significant relationship to juvenile chronic maladaptive behavior.

TABLE 19

Is Parent Consistent in Disciplining the Juvenile? by

Chronic and Nonchronic Maladaptive Behavior, Parent's

Age 31-40

		CHRONBEH		
Count				Row
Row Pct		Nonchronic	Chronic	Total
		1.00	2.00	
No	0	25	35	60
		41.7	58.3	85.7
Yes	1	09	01	10
		90.0	10.0	14.3
Column		34	36	70
Total		48.6	51.4	100.0

TABLE 20

Is Juvenile Involved in Cultural and Ethnic Activities? by

Chronic or Nonchronic Maladaptive Behavior, Parent's

Age 31-40

		CHRONBEH		
Count Row Pct		Nonchronic 1.00	Chronic 2.00	Row Total
No	0	28 43.1	37 56.9	65 91.5
Yes	1	06 100.0	00 00.0	06 08.5
Column Total		34 47.9	36 52.1	70 100.0

Table 19 shows that when the parent's consistency in disciplining the juvenile was tested for chronic or nonchronic behavior, controlling for the computed age of the parents between the ages of 31 and 40, their children exhibited less chronic maladaptive behavior (90% nonchronic). Furthermore, the test of statistical significance revealed a chi-square value of 6.20, which makes Hypothesis 1 statistically significant at the 0.01 level (p < 0.01).

Table 20 shows that among parents 31 to 40 years of age with children involved in cultural and ethnic activities, the children exhibited hardly any chronic maladaptive behavior. Moreover, the test of statistical significance revealed a chi-square value of 5.03, which makes Hypothesis 1 statistically significant at the 0.02 level (p < 0.02).

> *Hypothesis 2:* The majority of single African-American females who are heading households in which juveniles exhibit chronic maladaptivity are not afforded the inherent strengths of their natural support systems.

Table 21 and 22 shows that the Hypothesis 2 is supported: when natural support items are controlled in the multivariate analysis of chronic or nonchronic behavior and interpersonal bonding factors, the lack of natural (in-home) support systems was found to be significant in two of the interpersonal bonding factors: parent preparing and sharing meals with the juvenile, and the parent contacting the agency willingly.

Hypothesis 2 is supported further in significant relationships where the source of natural support was a nonrelative (significant other) (see Table 23). The children of the parents who contacted the agency willingly and who had no natural support exhibited more chronic maladaptive behavior than children of parents who did not contact the agency willingly. In the cases of the parents who failed to give their child one-on-one time and who lacked any natural support, the incidence of maladaptive behavior was higher. In the cases of parents with nonrelatives (live-in significant others) who did not prepare or share meals with the juveniles the frequency of maladaptive behavior among their children was alarmingly high (85%) (see Table 21). This trend also appeared among the parents who were not consistent in disciplining their children.

TABLE 21

Does Parent Prepare and Share Meals with Juvenile? by

Chronic and Nonchronic Maladaptive Behavior,

Nonrelative

		CHRONBEH		
Count Row Pct		Nonchronic 1.00	Chronic 2.00	Row Total
No	0	02 15.4	11 84.6	13 72.2
Yes	1	04 85.0	04 20.0	05 27.8
Column Total		06 33.3	12 66.7	18 100.0

TABLE 22

Did Parent Contact Agency Willingly? by Chronic and Nonchronic Maladaptive Behavior, No Support

---

		CHRONBEH		
Count Row Pct		Nonchronic 1.00	Chronic 2.00	Row Total
No	0	16 32.7	33 67.3	49 46.2
Yes	1	32 56.1	25 43.9	57 53.8
Column Total		48 45.5	58 54.7	106 100.0

TABLE 23

Relationships of Interpersonal Bonding Factors to Chronic

Maladaptivity, Controlling for Parent's Characteristics

	Chi Square	df	p	Tau	p	N
Age of Parent (31-40)						
Is parent consistent in disciplining the juvenile?	6.20	1	.013	-.34	.003	70
Is juvenile involved in cultural/ethnic activities?	5.03	1	.025	-.32	.004	71
Unemployed Parents						
Did parent contact agency willingly?	8.20	1	.004	-.31	.001	96
Does parent prepare/ share meals with juvenile?	3.81	1	.051	-.22	.015	98
Is parent consistent in disciplining the juvenile?	2.74	1	.098	-.20	.027	97
Employed Parents						
Is the parent willing to trust the child?	3.51	1	.061	-.42	.013	29
Primary Source of Income (AFDC)						
Did parent contact agency willingly?	6.35	1	.012	-.30	.003	85

*Primary Source of Income
(Other)*
Does parent give juvenile
one-to-one time?   *   1   .077 -.53 .012 15
Does parent listen to
communicate w/juvenile?   *   1   .01   -.73 .003 15

*Secondary Source of
Income (Other)*
Did parent contact
agency willingly?   *   -- .048 -.79 .000   9

*Secondary Source of
Income (Soc. Sec.)*
Does parent listen to
and communicate with
juvenile?   *   -- .029 -.71 .005 14

Parents Never Married
Did parent contact
agency willingly?   5.31 1   .021 -.27 .006 87

No Natural Support
Did parent contact
agency willingly?   4.96 1   .026 -.23 .008 106

*"Natural" Support is
Non-Relative*
Does parent prepare/
share meals with juvenile? *   -- .022 -.61 .006 18
Is parent consistent in
disciplining the juvenile? *   -- .083 -.47 .026 18

---

* Fisher's Exact

CHAPTER VIII

SUMMARY AND DISCUSSION OF FINDINGS

In this investigation I examined several factors that are considered to influence juvenile chronic maladaptive behavior in African-American female-headed households. I hypothesized that the interpersonal attachment (bonding) between the parent and the juvenile would be associated significantly with such behavior. I hypothesized further that a significant relationship would exist between juvenile chronic maladaptivity and the lack of natural (in-home) support systems. In this chapter I summarize and discuss the principal findings, the limitations of the investigation, and the implications for social control theory, as well as making recommendations for future investigation.

Control theories (more specifically, social control theory) were supported by the findings stated in the two previous chapters. Both of the hypothesized relationships produced from social control theory were found to be statistically significant, although not overwhelmingly so. As demonstrated in Chapter VII, eight explanatory variables supported the conjectural frameworks and were statistically significant at or below the 0.10 level.

The finding concerning the parent's source of income, which showed that the primary source of income for the parents was Aid to Families with Dependent Children (AFDC), was consistent with previous findings

119

that propose a "feminization of poverty" and suggest that African-American female-headed households receiving welfare assistance are most conducive to generating juvenile delinquency or chronic maladaptive behavior (Black News Digest, 1985; Moynihan, 1965; U.S. Dept. of Labor, 1985).

The findings regarding the interpersonal bonding factors support other findings which propose that family process variables are associated directly with serious and chronic delinquency (Cernkovich & Giordano, 1987; Hirschi, 1969; Hirschi & Gottfredson, 1983; Patterson, 1980, 1982). These findings also support the recent research showing that socialization variables concerning direct parent-child relationships are the strongest prognosticators for the conduct of juveniles (Loeber & Stouthamer-Loeber, 1986). In addition, this investigation corroborates the findings produced from the Glueck and Glueck (1950) investigation, which focused on such family variables as supervision, attachment, and discipline. The findings relative to the natural (in-home) support systems supported previous literature, which reported that the single mother's separation from parents, siblings, and significant others creates conditions in which maladaptive behavior may be exhibited. This isolated situation also can result in the lack of information regarding significant social services and resources (Straus, Gelles, & Steinmetz, 1980).

Limitations of the Study

This investigation has several limitations. The first and perhaps the most critical limitation concerns the population of the study. The juveniles observed here cannot be regarded as representing all chronic maladaptive juveniles because of sampling bias: all of these juveniles had been referred to the agency's Early Attention Program. This agency's clientele consists of referrals with particular demographic, economic, and cultural attributes. Because many of the clients requesting assistance from the Children's Aid Society are of low socioeconomic status, this investigation did not include juveniles and single parents at higher levels, who might have sought assistance from private facilities.

Race is another very important limitation. The goal of this investigation was to determine specific elements that influence juvenile chronic maladaptive behavior in female-headed African-American households. Therefore it is not possible to generalize these findings to other minorities or to whites. Even so, this investigation provides the research community with valuable information about the interaction of single African-American mothers with their children.

Implications for Social Control Theory

This investigation supports social control theory very strongly in identifying family interactions that function as controls against juvenile chronic maladaptive behavior. Bivariate and multivariate relationships between single African-American females heading households and juvenile chronic maladaptive behavior are significant. The broad perspective of social control theory from which I obtained the social control (bonding) variables proved productive. Significant relationships between several of the interpersonal bonding factors and juvenile chronic maladaptive behavior, together with some significant relationships between the interpersonal bonding factors, juvenile chronic maladaptive behavior, and natural support systems suggest that internal family dynamics are important in influencing such behavior.

Social control theory is the most appropriate framework for explaining the complicated effects of bonding factors between the single African-American females heading households and their children; these effects are mediated by family interactions. Possibly research that assesses the influence of these bonding variables in relation to the juveniles' chronic maladaptive behavior will help to support other opinions regarding social control theory and will contribute to the current literature on family and juvenile behavior.

Recommendations for Future Research

This study confirmed the findings of other research: in female-headed homes, control, supervision, and communication are very important and tend to be related significantly to juvenile maladaptive behavior in almost all families. Cernkovich and Giordano (1987) found that communication was the most accurate predictor for delinquency among white juveniles, while control and supervision were considered most accurate among nonwhite juveniles. Further investigations are needed to determine more clearly the influence of control, supervision, and both verbal and nonverbal communication on African-American juveniles.

Nonverbal communication has received very little attention in criminological investigations.

In regard to the feminization of poverty discussed in this study and the fact that the primary source of income for the single mothers (69%) was Aid to Families with Dependent Children, further research is needed to ascertain how much, if any, financial assistance is received from the absent father. We have evidence that the number of African-American males who previously had the economic means to support their children has diminished at virtually the same rate at which African-American female-headed families have increased (Nichols-Casebolt, 1988). Perhaps future research on the high rate of African-American male unemployment would effect a change in policy, which eventually would relieve African-American females from assuming most of the financial responsibility for the children.

In addition, I recommend a follow-up investigation to ascertain whether the interpersonal bonding factor and/or the natural support systems continue to have more or less influence on juvenile chronic maladaptive behavior. This study has furnished significant information on the factors that influence bonding between the juvenile and the mother in the African-American family; a follow-up investigation could help to determine the conditions in which the bonding process between the juveniles and their single mothers increases or decreases.

The use of secondary data restricted me to employing information that had been collected for other reasons; therefore it weakened my capacity to evaluate the points of concern. Accordingly I recommend that future researchers in this area use other types of data.

Research on sibling relationships in the female-headed family could offer additional insight into juvenile chronic maladaptivity in African-American families. Several social scientists have noted that a child's position in the family (eldest, middle, or youngest) influences his or her ability to bond with the parent(s) and siblings living in the household. Sibling rivalry also has been suggested as affecting family dynamics (Baker, 1977). It is speculated that this rivalry could influence very directly the occurrence of juvenile chronic maladaptive behavior. I collected some data on siblings during this investigation; because the documentation was sporadic, however, I could not use the data in this inquiry. Perhaps a study focusing on sibling variables could help to advance our knowledge of family relationships and juvenile chronic maladaptive behavior. In addition, it could assist mental health professionals and law enforcement agencies in identifying the factors connected with this relationship and thereby could enhance intervention techniques.

Bonding affected some antisocial behaviors but not others. Because of the nature of the data available, I did not take into account individual differences due to genetic background and brain structure or differences due to learning and experience. For example, the fact that individuals showing poor school performance scored high in bonding might mean that such individuals had major problems involving learning disabilities, dyslexia, or hyperactivity.

I recommend further that future research include the theoretical considerations of biological behaviorism. This research would allow the investigator to focus on biological and individual differences between adaptive and maladaptive juveniles. C. Ray Jeffery (1965) was one of the first behaviorists to introduce the notion of learned criminal behavior by suggesting a connection between Skinnerian operant conditioning and crime. He and others have suggested various approaches regarding maladaptive behavior and biology (Nietzel, 1979).

The criminological literature today contains many references to the connection between biology and crime, including learning disorders, hypoglycemia, psychopathy, brain disorders in the frontal temporal lobes, brain injuries, and trauma to the neurotransmitter system (Conrad & Dinitz, 1977; Farrington, 1977; Fishbein, 1981; Fisbein & Thatcher, 1982; Ginsburg & Carter, 1987; Hamparian, 1978; Jeffery, 1979; Mednick, 1982). Future research should focus on the role of personality and individual differences as they influence bonding.

Finally, another major area of concern is a closer theoretical integration of the bonding process with the natural support system.

Summary and Conclusions

Much of the research on family and juvenile conduct relates to the concept of attachment or lack of attachment in single-parent or intact families. The purpose of this study was to examine more closely the factors considered by mental health professionals to influence the conditions in which juvenile chronic maladaptive behavior occurred in female-headed African-American female-headed households.

The population investigated here included 140 maladaptive juveniles who were referred to the Early Attention Program of Detroit's Children's Aid Society between 1984 and 1987. This cross-sectional exploratory investigation focused on secondary data analysis of interview records used by the case worker of the Children's Aid Society. I developed and used a codebook for coding the data and employed univariate, bivariate and multivariate analysis in analyzing the data.

The findings produced by this inquiry showed that my two hypotheses were supported by the data. More chronic maladaptive behavior was displayed by juveniles between 11 and 20 years of age when the parents did not contact the agency willingly; less such behavior occurred among male juveniles whose parents contacted the agency willingly. The leading interpersonal bonding factors among parents were contacting the agency willingly, being consistent in disciplining their children, and preparing and sharing meals with their children. The children of these parents tended to display less chronic maladaptive behavior than other juveniles in the study.

In regard to serious and nonserious maladaptive behavior and levels of bonding, the juveniles who exhibited first occurrences of maladaptive behavior had two to six bonding factors, indicating a smaller degree of marginal-level bonding. Two juveniles, however, showed 13 or 14 factors; this finding calls into question the validity of self-report data. Among juveniles exhibiting nonserious behavior, bonding factors ranged from 0 to 15.

Sixty juveniles had no second occurrences of maladaptivity. Those who exhibited second occurrences of serious maladaptive behavior had 0 to 6 bonding factors, suggesting low to marginal bonding. Among the nonserious maladaptive juveniles, the number of factors ranged from 0 to 6. When the first and second occurrences of maladaptive behavior were combined, the serious juveniles had a low to marginal number of bonding factors. This finding suggests that when bonding decreases, serious maladaptive behavior increases. In contrast, the nonserious juveniles had more (0-15) bonding factors, suggesting that when bonding is dispersed evenly, serious maladaptive behavior decreases.

In regard to natural support systems, the lack of a natural (in-home) support system was found to be significant in two of the interpersonal bonding factors. When parents failed to give their children one-on-one time and when they lacked any natural support, the incidence of maladaptive behavior was higher. The percentage of children exhibiting maladaptive behavior was alarmingly high in households where parents with nonrelatives (live-in significant others) as natural support did not prepare or share meals with the juveniles. The same situation applied to parents who were not consistent in disciplining their children.

It is important to note that the findings and conclusions reached in this investigation apply specifically to a population of African-American juveniles and their parents living in the Detroit area. I recognize that different results may emerge among other types of juveniles, such as violent, rural, or white subjects. These findings, however, can be useful to the research community in assessing the relationship of family functioning to various types of maladaptive behavior across diversified populations and cultures.

From a policy standpoint, this research may prove helpful for professionals in intervention with at-risk African-American juveniles. Early intervention to control delinquency, school problems, and other maladaptive behaviors can be based on both the bonding and the natural support systems in such families. This intervention can be made part of a general prevention program, which can include neurological assessments, drug therapies, and other psychosocial approaches.

A word of caution: the findings of this study may apply only to African-American households headed by single females. Cultural differences must be kept in mind in creating and coordinating policy efforts.

REFERENCES

Anderson, R.E. (1968). Where's dad? parental deprivation and delinquency. *Archives of General Psychiatry*, 18, 641-649.

Andrew, J.M. (1978). Violence among delinquents by family intactness and size. *Social Biology*, 23, 243-250.

Apalachee Mental Health Center. (1986). *Crisis intervention pamphlet.* Tallahassee: State of Florida.

Austin, R.L. (1978). Race, father-absence and female delinquency. *Criminology*. 15, 487-504.

Babbie, E. (1983). *The practice of social research.* Belmont, CA: Wadsworth.

Bahr, S.J., Bowerman, C., & Gecas, V. (1974). Adolescent perception of conjugal power. *Social Forces*, 52, 357-367.

Baker, F. (1977). The interface between professional and natural support systems. *ClinicalSocial Work Journal*, 2, 582-593.

Barkley, R.A., Ullman, D.G., Otto, L., & Brecht, J.M. (1977). The effect of sex typing and sex appropriateness of model behavior on children's limitation. *Child Depelopment*, *43*, 721-725.

Billingsley, A. (1968). *Black families in white America.* New York: Prentice-Hall.

Blassingame, J. (1972). *The slave community.* New York: Oxford University Press.

Bordua, D. (1962). Some comments on theories of group delinquency. *Sociological Inquiry*. 32: 245-260.

Canter, R.J. (1982). Family correlates of male and female delinquency. *Criminology*, *20*, 149-167.

Cashion, B.G. (1982). Female-headed families: Effects on children and clinical implications. *Journal of Marital and Family Therapy*, 20,77-85.

Cernkovich, S.A. & Giordano, P.C. (1987). Family relationships and delinquency. *Criminology*. 25,295-319.

Chilton, R.J., & Markle, G.E. (1972). Family disruption, delinquenct conduct and the effect of subclassification. *American Sociological Review*. 37, 93-99.

Clarke, S.H., & Koch, G.G. (1957). A study of self reported delinquency in Charlotte/Mecklenberg. *Popular Government*. 22, 37-43.Cloward, R.A., & Ohlin, L.E. (1960).

Cloward, R.A., & Ohlin, L.E. (1960). *Delinquency and opportunity*. New York: Free Press.

Cohen, A.K. (1955). *Delinquent boys*. New York: Free Press.

Conrad, J., & Dinitz, S. (1977). *In fear of each other*. Lexingtion, MA: Lexington Books.

Compton, B., & Gallaway, B. (1979). *Social work processes*. Ontario: Dorsey.

Devore, W. (1983). Ethnic reality: the life model and work with black families. *Social Casework*, *64*, 525-531.

Elliott, D.S., Ageton, S.S., & Canter, R.J. (1979). An integrated theoretical perspective on delinquent behavior. *J. Res. Crime and Delinquency*, *16*, 3-27.

Empey, L. (1987). American Delinquency: Its meaning and construction. Homewood, IL: Dorsey.

Farnsworth, M. (1984). Family structure, family attributes, and delinquency in a sample of low income, minority males and females. *Journal of Youth and Adolescence, 13,* 349-363.

Farrington, D.P., Ohlin, L.E., & Wilson, J.Q. (1986). *Understanding and controlling crime.* New York: Springer-Verlag.

Fishbein, D. (1981). *The contribution of refined carbohydrate consumption to maladaptive behavior.* Paper presented at the annual meeting of the American Society of Criminology, Washington, DC.

Fishbein, D., & Thatcher, R. (1982). Nutritional and electrophysiological indices of maladaptive behavior. In R. Wurtman and H. Lieberman (eds.), *Proceedings of the Center for Brain Sciences and Metabolism,* Cambridge: MIT.

Free, M.D. (1991). Clarifying the relationship between the broken home and juvenile delinquency: A critique of the current literature. *Deviant Behavior;* 12(2), 109-167.

Germain, C. B., & Gitterman, (1980). *The life model of social work practice.* New York: Columbia University Press.

Ginsburg, B.E., & Carter, B.F. (1987). *Premenstrual syndrome.* New York: Plenum.

Giordano, P.C. & Cernkovich, S.A. (1979). On complicating the relationship between liberation and delinquency. *Social Problems.* 26, 467-481.

Giordano, P.C., Cernkovich, S.A., & Pugh, M.D. (1985). Friendships and delinquency. *American Journal of Sociology, 91,* 170-202.

Glueck, S., & Glueck, E. (1950). *Unraveling Juvenile delinquency.* New York: Commonwealth Fund.

Glueck, S., & Glueck, E. (1961). *Family environment and delinquency*. London: Routledge and Kegan Paul.

Glick, P.C. (1979). Future American families. *Cofo Memo II, 3*, 1-3.

Gove, W.R., & Crutchfield, R.D. (1982). The family and juvenile delinquency. *Sociological Quarterly, 23*, 301-319.

Gordan, J. (1965). The poor of harlem: Social functioning in the underclass. New York: Prentice-Hall.

Guttman, H. (1976). *The black family in slavery and freedom*, 1750-1925. New York: Pantheon.

Hagen, F. (1982). *Research methods in criminal justice and criminology*. New York: Macmillan.

Hamparian, D.M. (1978). *The violent few*. Lexington, MA: Lexington Books.

Hennessy, M., Richard, P.J., & Beck, R.A. (1978). Broken homes and middle class delinquency. *Criminology* 15, 505-528.

Herzog, E., & Sudia, C.E. (1970). *Boys in fatherless homes*. Washington, DC: U.S. Dept. of Health, Education, and Welfare

Herzog, E., & Sudia, C.E. (1973). Children in fatherless families. *Review of Child Development Research*, 3:141-232.

Hess, R. & Shipman, V. (1965). Early experience and the socialization of cognitive modes in children. *Child Development*. 36: 869-886.

Hindelang, M.J. (1973). Causes of delinquency: A partial replication and extension. *Social Problems, 20*, 471-487.

Hirschi, Travis. (1969). *Causes of delinquency*. Berkeley: University of California Press.

Hirschi, T., & Gottfredson, M. (1983). Age and the explanation of crime. *American Journal of Sociology, 84*, 552-584.

Jeffery, C.R. (1977). *Crime prevention through environmental design*. Beverly Hills: Sage.

Jeffery. C.R. (1979). *Biology and crime*. Beverly Hills: Sage.

Jeffery, C.R. (1990). *Criminology: An interdisciplinary approach*. Englewood Cliffs, NJ: Prentice-Hall.

Kellam, S.G., Adams, R.G., Brown, H.C. and Esminger, M.E. (1982). The long term evolution of the family structure of teenage and older mothers. *Journal of Marriage and the Family* 44: 539-544.

LaGrange, R.L., & White, H.R. (1985). Age differences in delinquency: A test of theory. *Criminology, 23*, 19-45.

Lang, D., Pampenfuhs, R., & Walter, J. (1976). Delinquent females' perception of their fathers. *The Family Coordinator. 25*, 475-481.

Laub, J.H., & Sampson, R.J. (1987). Criminal careers and crime control: A matched sample, longitudinal research design. *Crime Control Theory and Policy Program*.

LeFlore, L. (1988). Delinquent youths and Family. *Adolescence*, 23(91), 629-642.

Levin, J. (1977). *Elementary statistics in social Research*. New York: Harper and Row.

Liska, A.E. (1981). *Perspectives on deviance*. Englewood Cliffs, NJ: Prentice-Hall.

Loeber, R., & Stouthamer-Loeber, M. (1986). Family factors as correlates and predictors of juvenile conduct, problems and delinquency. *Crime and Justice, An Annual review of Research*. Chicago: University of Chicago Press.

Longabough, R. (1973). Mother's behavior as a variable moderating the effects of father absence. *Ethos*, 14, 22-30.

Lueptow, L.B. (1980). Social structure, social change and parental influence and adolescent sex-role socialization: 1974-1975. *Journal of Marriage and the Family*, 42.

Maccoby, E.E. (1966). *The development of sex difference*. Palo Alto: Stanford University Press.

Mayfield-Brown, L. (1989). Family status of low income adolescene mothers Special Issue: Black Adolescents. *Journal of Adolescent Research*, 4(2), 202-213.

McClave, J., & Dietrich, F. (1985). *Statistics*. San Francisco: Dillen.

McGhee, J.D. (1984). A profile of the black single female-headed household. *The state of black America* (pp. 43-55). New York: National Urban League.

Mednick, S.A. (1982). Biology and violence. In M. Wolfgang & N. Weiner (Eds.), *Criminal violence*. Beverly Hills: Sage.

Merton, R.K. (1938). *Social theory and social structure*. New York: Free Press.

Monahan, T. (1957). Family status and the delinquent child: A reappraisal and some new findings. *Social Forces*. 35, 250-258.

Moynihan, D.P. (1965). The Negro family: The case for national action. *The Moynihan report and the politics of controversy*. Washington, DC: U.S. Government Printing Office.

National Center for Juvenile Justice. (1982). *Delinquency in the United States*. Pittsburgh.

National Center for Juvenile Justice. (1985). *Delinquency in the United States*. Pittsburgh.

National Urban League, Inc. (1984). *The state of black America*. New York: National Urban League.

Nettler, G. (1978). *Explaining crime*. New York: McGraw-Hill.

Nichols-Casebolt, A.N. (1988). Black families headed by single mothers: Growing numbers and increasing poverty. *Social work*, 33, 306-313.

Nietzel, M.T. (1979). *Crime and its modification: A social learning perspective*. New York: Pergamon.

Nye, F.I. (1958). *Family relationships and delinquent behavior*. New York: Wiley.

Patterson, G.R. (1980). Children who steal. In Travis Hirschi and Michael Gottfredson (Eds.), *Understanding crime*. Beverly Hills: Sage.

Patterson, G.R. (1982). *Coercion family process*. Eugene: Castalia.

Peters, M., & de Ford, C. (1986). The solo mother. In *The black family: Essays and studies*, (pp. 164-172). New York: Wadsworth.

Rankin, J.H. (1983). The family context of delinquency. *Social Problems*. 30, 466-479.

Reckless, W.C. (1961). A new theory of delinquency and crime; *Federal Probation*. 25, 42-46.

Roberts, A. (1983). Strengthening families and natural support systems four offenders. *Social work in juvenile and criminal justice settings*, Springfield, IL: Thomas.

Robins, L.N., & Hill. (1966). Assessing the contributions of family structure class and peer groups to juvenile delinquency. *Journal of Criminal Law, Criminology, and Police Science*, 57, 325-334.

Rosen, L. (1970). Matriarchy and lower class Negro male delinquency. *Social Problems.* 17, 175-189.

Rosen, L. (1985). Family and delinquency: Structure or function? *Criminology,* 23, 553-573.

Rosen, L., & Neilson, K. (1978). The broken home and delinquency. In L. Savitz & N. Johnson (Eds.), *Crime in society.* New York: Wiley.

Rosen, L., & Neilson K. (1982). Broken homes. *Contemporary criminology.* New York: Wiley.

Rutter, M., & Giller, H. (1984). *Juvenile delinquency: Trends and perspectives.* New York: Guilford.

Savitz, L.D., & Johnston, N. (1978). *Crime in society.* New York: Wiley.

Sedman, M. (1960). *Tactics of scientific research.* New York: Basic Books.

Sellitz, C., Wrightman, L.S., & Cook, S.W. (1976). *Research methods in social relations.* New York: Holt, Rinehart, and Winston.

Shoemaker, D.J. (1984). *Theories of delinquency.* New York: Oxford University Press.

Smith, E. (1987). The Black family: Daniel Patrick Moynihan and the tangle of pathology revisited. Special Issue: Black America in the 1980s. *Humbold Journal of Social Relations,* 14(1-2), 281-305.

Spanier, G.B. (1980). Outsiders looking in. *Wilson Quarterly, 4,* 122-135.

Staples, R. (1985). Changes in black family structure: The conflict between family ideology and structure condition. *Journal of Marriage and the Family,* 47, 1005-1013.

Staples, R. & Mirande,. (1980). Racial and cultural variations among American families. *Journal of Marriage and The Family, 42,* 887-903.

Staples, R. (1971). Parental rules. *The black family* (pp. 393-405). Belmont, CA: Wadsworth.

Straus, N.A., Gelles, R.J., & Steinmetz, S.K. (1980). *Behind closed doors: Violence in the American family.* New York: Anchor.

Sykes, G.M., & Matza, D. (1957). Techniques of neutralization: A theory of delinquency. *American Sociological Review, 22 664-670.*

Taub, S., & Little, C.B. (1985). *Theories of deviance.* Washington, DC: U.S. Department of Labor.

U.S. Bureau of the Census. (1981). *Historical statistics of the united states.* Washington, DC: U.S. Government Printing Office.

U.S. Department of Justice. (1973, June). *Criminal Justice Monograph,* pp. 56-67.

U.S. Department of Justice. (1987). *Children in custody.*

U.S. Department of Justice. (1988). *Juvenile Justice Bulletin.*

U.S. Department of Labor. (1984a, October.). Dramatic growth of black female-headed families seen over last decade. *Black News Digest.*

U.S. Department of Labor. (1984b, August). The United Nations decade for women, 1976-1985: Employment in the United States. *Black News Digest.*

U.S. Department of Labor. (1985, October). Women who maintain families. *FACT SHEETS, Women's Bureau,* pp.7-10.

Vold, G.B., & Bernard, T.J. (1986). *Theoretical criminology.* New York: Oxford University Press.

Wells, L.E., & Rankin, J.H. (1985). Broken homes and delinquency: An empirical review. *Criminal Justice Abstracts, 17,* 249-272.

Wells, L.E., & Rankin, J.H. (1986). The broken home model of delinquency: Analytic issues. *Journal of Research in Crime and Delinquency, 23,* 68-93.

Wilkinson, K. (1974). The broken family and juvenile delinquency: Secientific explanation or ideology? *Social Problems, 21,* 726-739.

Wilkinson, K. (1980). The broken home and delinquent behavior: An alternative interpretation of contradictory findings. *Understanding crime: Current theory and research* (pp.144-154). Beverly Hills: Sage.

Willie, C.V. (1970). *The family life of black people.* Columbus, OH: Merrill.

Wilson, J. Q., & Herrnstein, R.J. (1985). *Crime and human nature.* New York: Simon and Schuster.

Wolfgang, M.E., Figlio, R., & Thornberg, T. (1978). *Evaluating criminology.* New York: Elsevier.

APPENDIX: DATA COLLECTION INSTRUMENT

DATA INFORMATION SHEET

Parent's Name _____

Child's Name _____

Case Number _____

Case Identification Number __ __ __

DEMOGRAPHIC VARIABLES ON THE PARENT(S)
Race __
1 = White
2 = Black
3 = Other
9 = Unknown

Sex __
0 = Male
1 = Female
9 = Unknown

Date of Birth __ __ __ __ __ __   (Age __ __)
(MMDDYY)
999999 = Unknown

Address __ __ __ __ __ __ __ __ __ __ __ __ __ __ __ __
9999999999999999 = Unknown

PARENTAL SOCIO-ECONOMIC VARIABLES

Employment __

0 = Employed
1 = Unemployed
9 = Unknown

Source of Income __ __

01=Interest income (savings, checking, dividends, real estate income, etc)
02=Employment income
03=Self-employment income
04=AFDC (Aid to Families With Dependent Children)
05=Other social service benefits (food stamps, Women, Infant and Children WIC)
06=VA (Veterans Administration)
07=Child support
08=Unemployment Compensation
09=Social Security
10=Other
99=Unknown

Second Source of Income __ __
(Coding same as above)

Education of Parent __ __

01=1-8 grades, Graduate, Degree
02=9-12 grades, Graduate, Degree
03=Tradeschool Graduate, Degree
04=College, Graduate (2 yr or 4 yr.) Degree
05=Professional School, Graduate, Degree
06=Other
09=Unknown

Parental Status __
1=Single
2=Separated
3=Divorced
4=Widowed
5=Guardian
6=Other
9=Unknown

"NATURAL" SUPPORT SYSTEM VARIABLES (OF SINGLE FEMALE PARENT)

Support System (living in household) Relationship To Parent __ __
01=Father
02=Mother
03=Both parents
04=Step mother
05=Step father
06=Sibling(s)
07=Other relative
08=Parent's live-in boyfriend/girlfriend
09=Other
10=None indicated
99=Unknown

INCIDENT(S) OF PARENTAL CRIMINAL CONVICTIONS

Type of Criminal Behavior __
1=Assault
2=Robbery
3=Burglary
4=Theft

5=Forgery
6=Drugs
7=Other
8=None indicated
9=Unknown

Second Type of Criminal Convictions __
(Coding same as above)

Time received __ __
01=Less than 5 years
02=More than 5 years
09=Unknown

Fine received __ __
01=Less than $500
02=More than $500
09=Unknown

Reconviction __
1=None
2=One
3=Two or more
9=Unknown

DEMOGRAPHIC VARIABLES ON THE JUVENILE

Race __
1=White
2=Black
3=Other
9=Unknown

Sex __
0=Male
1=Female
2=Unknown

Date of Birth __ __ __ __ __ __
(MMDDYY)
999999=Unknown

Address __ __ __ __ __ __ __ __ __ __ __ __ __ __ __ __
999999999999999=Unknown

Employment __
0=Employed
1=Unemployed
9=Unknown

Education of Juvenile __ __
01=1-8 grade, Graduate, Degree
02=9-12 grade, Graduate, Degree
03=Tradeschool, Graduate, Degree
04=Other
09=Unknown

INCIDENT(S) OF JUVENILE MALADAPTIVE BEHAVIOR

TYPE OF MALADAPTIVE BEHAVIOR __
1=Shoplifting
2=Run-a-way
3=Truancy
4=Other
9=Unknown

Second Type of Maladaptive Behavior __
1=Shoplifting
2=Run-a-way
3=Truancy
4=Other
9=Unknown

Date of Maladaptive Behavior __ __ __ __ __ __
(MMDDYY)
999999=Unknown

CASE REPORT VARIABLES
Case Reported By __ __
01=Law Enforcement
02=Neighbor
03=Friend
04=Child/Victim (self-referral)
05=Parent
06=Other relative
07=School employee
08=Social Service Agency employee
09=Medical personnel
10=Mental Health Personnel
11=Court personnel
12=Clergy
13=Anonymous
14=Other
99=Unknown

Case Reported To __
1=Police
2=WCJC (Wayne County Juvenile Court)
3=Children's Aid Society (CAS)
4=Both (Police and CAS)

5=Both (WCJC and CAS)
6=Other
7=Unknown

Date Report Received By The CAS __ __ __ __ __ __
(MMDDYY)
999999=Unknown

Date Investigation Started __ __ __ __ __ __
(MMDDYY)
999999=Unknown

Date Investigation Closed __ __ __ __ __ __
(Official Closure Date of Report)
(MMDDYY)
999999=Unknown

DEMOGRAPHIC VARIABLES ON OTHER CHILDREN WITHIN THE HOUSEHOLD

Second Child's Race __
1=Black
2=White
3=Other
4=Unknown

Second Child's Sex __
0=Male
1=Female
9=Unknown

Third Child's Race __
1=Black
2=White
3=Other
4=Unknown

Third Child's Sex __
0=Male
1=Female
9=Unknown

Fourth Child's Race __
(Coding same as above)

Fourth Child's Sex __
(Coding same as above)

Second Child's Date of Birth __ __ __ __ __ __
(MMDDYY)
999999=Unknown

Third Child's Date of Birth __ __ __ __ __ __
(Coding same as above)

Fourth Child's Date of Birth __ __ __ __ __ __
(Coding same as above)

INTERPERSONAL INTERACTION OF PARENT WITH JUVENILE

Did the parent contact the agency willingly? __ __
00=Yes
01=No
09=Unknown

Does the juvenile have a curfew? __ __
00=Yes
01=No
09=Unknown

Does the parent attend parent/teacher conference and other school activities? __ __
00=Yes
01=No
09=Unknown

Does the parent assist juvenile with homework? __ __
00=Yes
01=No
09=Unknown

Does the parent give the juvenile one on one personal time? __ __
00=Yes
01=No
09=Unknown

Does the parent prepare meals and or share meals with the juvenile? __ __
00=Yes
01=No
09=Unknown

Does the parent and juvenile attend religious services?

__ __
00=Yes
01=No
09=Unknown

Is the parent consistent in disciplining the juvenile?

$\overline{00}=\overline{\text{Yes}}$
01=No
09=Unknown

	*N	AN	O	AA	A
Does the parent encourage the juvenile to participate in family decision making (allowing juvenile to feel some control over his/her life)?	1	2	3	4	5
Is the parent willing to trust the child?	1	2	3	4	5
Is the parent willing to listen to and communicate with the juvenile?	1	2	3	4	5
Is the parent involved in leisure time activities within the juvenile?	1	2	3	4	5
Is the juvenile involved in cultural/ethnic activities within the community?	1	2	3	4	5
Is the juvenile's television and movie selections monitored by the parent?	1	2	3	4	5

Is the parent involved in
the juvenile's medical and
dental care program?   1   2   3   4   5

*N	=	NEVER
AN	=	ALMOST NEVER
O	=	OCCASIONALLY
AA	=	ALMOST ALWAYS
A	=	ALWAYS

Panel of Judges:
Dr. Juanita Doss (Psychologist)
Dr. Michelle Reid (Psychiatrist)
Mr. William Iverson (Social Worker)

INCIDENT(S) OF ALCOHOL ABUSE

Parent abuses alcohol __ __
01=Yes
02=No
03=Alcoholic
09=Unknown

Special Notes

Juvenile abuses alcohol __ __
1=Yes
2=No
3=Alcoholic
4=Under influence of alcohol during offense
9=Unknown

Special Notes

INCIDENT(S) OF DRUG ABUSE

Parent abuses drugs __ __
01=Yes
02=No
03=Drug Addict
09=Unknown

Special Notes

Juvenile abuses drugs __
1=Yes
2=No
3=Drug Addict
4=Under influence of drugs during offense
9=Unknown

Special Notes

INCIDENT(S) OF SPOUSE ABUSE
Type of Abuse __
1=Physical abuse
2=Emotional abuse
3=Neglect
4=Other
5=None indicated
9=Unknown

Special Notes

Incident(s) of Juvenile Abuse
Type of abuse __
1=Sexual abuse
2=Physical abuse

3=Emontional abuse
4=Neglect
5=Other
9=Unknown

Special Notes

Abuser's Relationship To Juvenile __ __
01=Father
02=Mother
03=Both parents
04=Stepfather
05=Sibling
06-Other relative
07=Babysitter
08=School employee
09=Child day care worker
10=Mother's live-in boyfriend
11=Stranger
12=Other
99=Unknown

Special Notes

SUPPORTING EVIDENCE OF ABUSE

Based On Eyewitness Statements __
0=Yes
1=No
9=Unknown

Special Notes

LEGAL ACTION

Adult Court __
0=Criminal charges filed
1=No criminal charges filed
9=Unknown

Juvenile Court __
0=Petition filed
1=No petition filed
9=Unknown

CASE DISPOSITION
Disposition __
1=Case closed (objectives completed)
2=Case closed (Lack of client participation)
3=Case still under investigation
4=Unable to locate
5=Undetermined
6=Other
9=Unknown
Removal of the Child was Required __
0=Yes
1=No
9=Unknown

Where Was The Child Placed If Removed __
(Leave blank if NO removal was required.)
1=Shelter
2=Relative
3=Foster home
4=Other
9=Unknown

INCIDENT(S) OF INVOLVEMENT WITH OTHER SOCIAL SERVICES
1=Department of Social Services
2=Protective Services
3=Wayne County Juvenile Court (WCJC)
4=Northwest Guidance Center
5=Neighbor Service Organization (NSO)
6=Catholic Social Services
7=None indicated
8=Other
9=Unknown

INDEX

Academic ability, 48
Adams, R.G., 23
Age
  of juveniles, 86, 88
  of parents, 36, 86
Ageton, S.S., 43
Aggressiveness, family
      structure and, 24
Anderson, R.E., 23
Andrew, J.M., 34, 37
Attachment, 43, 46
  to parents, 47
  to peers, 48
  to school, 47
Austin, R.L., 34, 37

Babbie, E., 56, 57, 75, 78, 104
Bahr, S.J., 43
Baker, F., 7, 124
Barkley, R.A., 33
Beck, R.A., 37
Belief, 42, 43, 47
Billingsley, A., 4, 27, 74
Biological behaviorism,
      need for research on,
      125
Biological pushes, 42
Bivariate analyses, 75, 78,
      99-103
Blassingame, J., 25

Bonding,
  incidence of, 88-91
  need for research on
      increases or decreases
      in, 123
Bordua, D., 16
Brecht, J.M., 33
Brown, H.C., 23

Canter, R.J., 16, 18, 43
Carter, B.F., 125
Cashion, B.G., 27, 32-35
Cernkovich, S.A., 8, 17, 37,
      120, 122
Children's Aid Society, 54-55
Chilton, R.J., 8, 23, 34, 37
Chronic Maladaptive
      Behavior Scale
      (CMBS), 76
Clarke, S.H., 23
Cloward, R.A., 8
Cohen, A.K., 8
Commitment, 42, 43, 46-47
Communication, need for
      research on, 122
Communication
      Questionnaire, 67
Compton, B., 68
Confidentiality, use of
      secondary data analysis
      and, 57

154